Aim for a top SATs mark with CGP!

If you're finding KS2 English a bit of a breeze, you'll really enjoy the challenge of this CGP Stretch Revision Book.

We've made sure all the toughest parts of KS2 English are easy to understand — with crystal-clear notes and examples to fully explain everything you need to know for the SATs.

There are also questions throughout to test what you've learned — with answers included for easy marking!

What CGP is all about

Our sole aim here at CGP is to produce the highest quality books — carefully written, immaculately presented and dangerously close to being funny.

Then we work our socks off to get them out to you — at the cheapest possible prices.

Contents

Published by CGP

Editors:
Chloe Anderson, Izzy Bowen, Emma Cleasby, Emma Crighton, Jack Perry, Rebecca Tate and Adam Worster

With thanks to Glenn Rogers and Matt Topping for the proofreading.
With thanks to Jan Greenway for the copyright research.

ISBN: 978 1 78294 679 3

Printed by Elanders Ltd, Newcastle upon Tyne.
Clipart from Corel®

Based on the classic CGP style created by Richard Parsons.

Text, design, layout and original illustrations © Coordination Group Publications Ltd. (CGP) 2019
All rights reserved.

Word Meaning

The different meanings of words can be confusing — you can use other words to help.

Some Questions Ask What Words Mean

1) You might be asked to <u>explain</u> what a word from the text means.

EXAMPLE: Use this sentence to explain the meaning of the word 'compassionate'.

Abigail is a very <u>compassionate</u> person, which is why the animals liked her.

In this sentence, '<u>compassionate</u>' means <u>caring</u>.

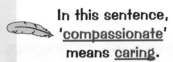

2) You could be asked to explain what the meaning of a word <u>suggests</u>.

EXAMPLE: What does the word 'bounded' suggest about the way Trixie moved?

'Bounded' tells you she <u>moved quickly</u>.

Trixie <u>bounded</u> over to see Sam and Fatima.

The Rest of the Sentence Might Help You

1) If you're unsure about the meaning of a word, use what's <u>around</u> it to help you.

EXAMPLE: What does the word 'ravenous' suggest about the cat?

The <u>ravenous</u> cat stared <u>longingly</u> at the plump, <u>delicious-looking</u> fish.

Words like '<u>longingly</u>' and '<u>delicious-looking</u>' help you to <u>work out</u> what the word means.

It's friendly. ☐   It's hungry. ☑

It's tired. ☐   It's angry. ☐

2) Some words can mean <u>different things</u> in <u>different sentences</u>, so you'll <u>need</u> to look at the <u>rest of the sentence</u> to work out what they mean.

Tony plays lots of <u>wind</u> instruments. ◄ Here, Tony is <u>playing</u> music, so 'wind' is a <u>type of musical instrument</u>.

The paths <u>wind</u> around the hills. ◄ In this sentence, 'wind' is a verb. It tells you the <u>layout</u> of the <u>paths</u>.

"I can understand and explain the meaning of words."

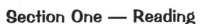

Retrieving Information

Reading texts are often full of useful information. You need to be able to dig it all up.

You Might Just Need to Find Information

1) Some questions just want you to <u>find information</u> in the text.

EXAMPLE: What did the doctor give to Amir?

This question just needs a <u>short</u>, simple answer.

2) Sometimes the answers might be <u>hard to find</u> in the text. <u>Scan</u> through the text looking for <u>words</u> from the <u>question</u>. This may <u>help</u> you find the <u>information</u>.

3) Some questions will ask you for <u>more than one</u> answer.

EXAMPLE: Write down two things you are told about the goat's eating habits.

Make sure you write the <u>correct number</u> of things. If you don't, you <u>won't</u> get the <u>marks</u>.

4) Sometimes you might be asked <u>why</u> something is happening or <u>how</u> you <u>know</u> something.

EXAMPLE: Give one reason why the clowns left.

5) Make sure you get your answer <u>from the text</u>. <u>Don't</u> be tempted to answer questions using your <u>own knowledge</u>.

You Might be Asked a True or False Question

You might have to <u>decide</u> if a statement is <u>true</u> or <u>false</u> based on what you've read in the text. <u>All</u> the <u>information</u> you need will be <u>in the text</u> — you just have to <u>find</u> it.

EXAMPLE: Read each sentence and tick one box to show whether it is true or false.

	True	False
Three-headed dragons are notoriously fierce.	☐	☐
The courageous knight battled with the dragon.	☐	☐

Make sure there is information in the text that <u>backs up</u> your answer.

"I can retrieve and record information and identify key details from the text."

Summarising

Summarising is all about finding the important information and main ideas in a text.

You Might Have to Summarise

1) Summary questions ask about information that's spread across different paragraphs.

2) You might have to say what the main message of a text is, say what a character is like or answer questions where the information isn't all in one place.

> **EXAMPLE:**
>
> One of the main ideas of the text is that Nigel the octopus is trying to sneak into the castle. Explain how this is shown in the text.
>
>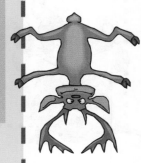
>
> The words in pink show Nigel was dishonest.
>
> The text mentions two attempts to get into the castle.
>
> Getting past the Guardfish was Nigel's only hope of entering the castle. Nigel had tried to deceive the first guard by claiming that he had urgent business with King Cod. The Guardfish had refused him entry and banished him from castle grounds.
>
> Nigel was persistent, and he devised a way to dupe the next Guardfish on duty. He disguised himself as a member of the kitchen staff to gain access to the tower.

Writing About Characters Can Be Tricky

1) You could be asked about a character — what they're like or how they behave.

2) Read the text and look for clues about that character. Think about how they react to situations or how they treat others.

> **EXAMPLE:**
>
> Which of the following best describes Harry?
> Find and copy a sentence or phrase which supports your answer.
>
> The underlined bits suggest he's full of energy.
>
> Harry stirred in his sleep, grumbled softly and slowly opened one eye. Seeing the sun seeping through the blinds, he scrambled out of bed and raced outside. He was determined to master a cartwheel.
>
> He scuttled towards the lawn, discarded his shoes and breathed deeply to ready himself. Arms outstretched, he launched himself forward with all his might. His legs sailed through the air... and then he could feel the strands of grass between his toes once more. Harry righted himself and, realising his achievement, dashed around the garden cheering.
>
> strong ☐   busy ☐   lazy ☐   energetic ☑

"I can summarise main ideas from more than one paragraph."

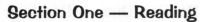

Making Inferences

Sometimes the meaning of a text isn't obvious — you need to read carefully to work it out.

Inferring Means Working Something Out

1) Sometimes writers <u>don't say</u> what they <u>mean</u> clearly. Instead they <u>suggest</u> something, and you have to <u>read between the lines</u> to work out the <u>meaning</u>.

2) For example, you might be asked to decide <u>how</u> a character <u>feels</u> about something.

> **EXAMPLE:** How does Becky feel about going into the abandoned house?
>
> Becky's hands were <u>trembling</u> as she opened the door. She <u>hesitated</u>, peering down the hallway, and <u>flinched</u> as a bird came flying out.
>
> These words show that Becky feels <u>nervous</u> about going into the house.

3) You might need to <u>back up</u> your answer with <u>evidence</u>. Use <u>details</u> from the text or <u>quotations</u> (the actual words from the text) to say <u>why</u> you think you're right.

Remember to put any quotations in speech marks.

> **EXAMPLE:**
> How can you tell that the bee was tired?
>
> The <u>drowsy</u> bee felt <u>drained</u> after heaving buckets of honey.

Words like '<u>drowsy</u>' and '<u>drained</u>' tell you the bee was <u>exhausted</u>.

You Need to Know About Facts and Opinions

You might need to say whether something is a <u>fact</u> or an <u>opinion</u>.

> **EXAMPLE:**
> Read each sentence and tick <u>one</u> box to show whether it is a <u>fact</u> or an <u>opinion</u>.

	Fact	Opinion
Blue whales are the largest animals on Earth.	✓	
Whales are interesting creatures.		✓

This sentence can be <u>backed up</u> with <u>evidence</u>. It's a <u>fact</u>.

This sentence tells you what someone <u>thinks</u>. It can't be <u>proved</u> with evidence. It's an <u>opinion</u>.

"I can make inferences and justify them with evidence from the text."

 ✓ ✓ ✓

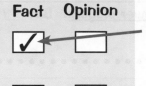

What Happens Next?

A good text makes you want to know what happens next — you may need to work it out...

You Might Have to Make a Prediction

1) You could be asked to <u>predict</u> what will happen next in a text based on <u>what you've read</u>.

2) Often you'll need to explain <u>why</u> you think it is going to happen.

EXAMPLE:	What do you think the mouse will do next?

3) <u>Before</u> you write down your answer, ask yourself these <u>questions</u>:

① What is <u>currently happening</u> at the <u>end</u> of the text?

② What is the overall <u>feeling</u>? Are the characters happy? Are they in danger?

③ What do you think is <u>likely</u> to happen next?

Your Prediction Must be Based on the Text

Make sure your prediction is <u>backed up</u> by the text — <u>don't</u> just make up anything.

> **EXAMPLE:**
>
> Do you think Alexa's team will win the match?
> Give a reason for your answer.
>
> > Alexa was <u>determined</u> to beat her rivals. A midfielder fired the ball in her direction and she took aim at the goal. The ball <u>rebounded</u> off the bar and the other team <u>gained control</u>. The pace quickened as the opposition swiftly passed the ball from player to player.
> >
> > Suddenly, the whistle sounded and a defender from the other team was <u>sent off</u>. <u>Alexa thrived on pressure</u>, and now it was <u>her chance to score the winning goal</u> while the other team had <u>fewer players</u>. But <u>time was running out</u>...

At first, Alexa is focused on <u>winning</u>.

However, she <u>misses</u> a chance to score a goal.

Then Alexa sees that they have a chance since they have <u>more players</u>.

The game is nearly over, so Alexa's team might not have <u>time</u> to score.

You can say yes <u>or</u> no, as long as there are <u>reasons</u> in the text to support your answer.

"I can predict what will happen next based on information in the text."

Structure

Structure is about where information goes in a text — the order that things come in.

Some Questions Ask About Structure

1) <u>Structure questions</u> are about <u>how</u> the information in a text <u>fits together</u>.

2) You could be asked to find the <u>point</u> in a text where something <u>important</u> happens. This could be the point where a person's <u>feelings suddenly change</u> or when the story swaps between locations.

EXAMPLE:

Find and copy one phrase which shows that Priya's feelings change.

> The peculiar sound was high-pitched and had a constant rhythm. It was coming from upstairs. Priya crept up cautiously, anxious about the unnerving sound. She was aware of a shuffling sound now too, in harmony with the squeaking. Priya slowly opened the door to her brother's room and <u>her worries melted away</u>. Her brother was looking after his friend's hamster while she was on holiday.

The phrase in blue shows how the <u>tension eases</u> when Priya realises it was just the <u>hamster</u> being noisy.

You Might Need to Put Things in Order

1) Some questions might ask you to put <u>events</u> in the right <u>order</u>.

2) Read through the text <u>carefully</u>, looking for <u>each event</u>.

3) If you're allowed to, <u>mark</u> each event on the <u>paper</u>.

4) Then fill in the <u>answers</u> in the right order.

Different Bits of the Text do Different Things

You might have to say what <u>function</u> part of a story has — what it <u>does</u> in the text.

The vast park was serene and deserted.	Character description	She soared over the puddle.	Background or past events	She would be more cautious in future.
↑ Description or setting	↓ Noelle was passionate about running.	↑ Action	↓ She sprained her ankle last summer.	↑ Moral or lesson

---

"I can explain how different parts of texts are related and describe the function of part of a text."

Section One — Reading

Choice of Language

Here's a page about the writer's choice of language and the sort of things you need to look for.

Some Questions Focus on Language

1) The language in a text has usually been chosen for a reason.

2) Make sure you can find words which describe things in a certain way.

EXAMPLE: Find and copy three words that show Dr Grater is a villain.

Look for words that are associated with the word 'villain'.

> Once again, Edam McStilton narrowly dodged the evil Dr Grater's grasp. The plucky hero was used to being pursued by the fiendish and devious doctor, and he always managed to evade capture. However, his chances of escaping began to fade as the gates swung closed. Dr Grater let out a wicked cackle. Edam was trapped.

There might be lots of answers to choose from, but you only need to give the number you're asked for.

Language Can Tell You What Things are Like

1) You might also need to explain what a word or phrase from the text tells you.

2) Think about the overall impression the text gives you and how different words and phrases make you feel about what's being described.

EXAMPLE: What does this paragraph tell you about Finn?

The words in green show that Finn is an excellent and dedicated singer.

> Finn dreamt of being an opera singer. The cellar was his stage and he would put on exquisite performances to an audience of one (in front of the mirror). He would repeatedly practise the array of songs he had learned over the years, polishing each piece to perfection. However, he hid his aspirations from his family, falling silent each time he heard footsteps treading above. His singing was limited to the few hours a week that he was alone in the house.

The words in pink tell you Finn is afraid of his secret being revealed.

"I can identify how language can affect meaning."

Comparing

Comparing is about finding the similarities and differences between two things.

Some Questions Ask How Things Compare

1) You might get a question that asks you to compare how two things are <u>similar</u> or <u>different</u>.

2) Look at the <u>information</u> that is given about both things to decide on your answer.

> **EXAMPLE:**
>
> How does Harriet's life on the island of Orpa compare with her life on Wado?

Look out for <u>key words</u> that give you an idea of how they're the <u>same</u> or <u>different</u>.

> Orpa was rugged with endless scenic views. It was <u>isolated</u>, but Harriet enjoyed the <u>tranquillity</u> and <u>stillness</u> this provided. She revelled in being able to read outside without the <u>drone</u> of traffic in the background. Her five years living on Wado had been a <u>whirlwind</u> of <u>bustling city life</u>. The <u>leisurely</u> pace of life on Orpa was a welcome change.

Wado is <u>noisy</u> and <u>hectic</u>.   Orpa, on the other hand, is <u>relaxed</u> and <u>peaceful</u>.

3) If the question asks for a <u>certain number</u> of similarities or differences, make sure that's the number you <u>write</u>. Otherwise you'll <u>miss out</u> on <u>marks</u>!

You Could be Asked How Things Change

1) You might also be asked how something <u>changes</u>, for example a character's mood.

2) Look at the <u>beginning</u> and <u>end</u> of the bit you're asked about, and write about any <u>differences</u> between the two.

Some comparison questions may focus on <u>one part</u> of the text.

> **EXAMPLE:**
>
> At the beginning of the text, Naima is afraid to go diving. How is her character different at the end of the text?

Look for <u>information</u> towards the <u>end</u> of the text about how Naima feels about diving.

"I can make comparisons within texts."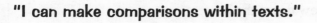

Practice Questions — Fiction

Read this extract from a story, then answer the questions below.

This is an extract from *The Coral Island: A Tale of the Pacific Ocean* by R. M. Ballantyne, written in 1858. The narrator, Ralph, has been shipwrecked on an island in the Pacific Ocean, along with his friends, Jack and Peterkin. After many days stranded on the island, Peterkin sees a boat sailing towards them.

The Coral Island

"A sail! a sail! Ralph, look! Jack, away on the horizon there, just over the entrance to the lagoon!" cried Peterkin, as we scrambled up the rocks.

"So it is, and a schooner*, too!" said Jack, as he proceeded hastily to dress.

Our hearts were thrown into a terrible flutter by this discovery, for if it should touch at our island we had no doubt the captain would be happy to give us a passage to some of the civilized islands, where we could find a ship sailing for England, or some other part of Europe. Home, with all its associations, rushed in upon my heart like a flood, and, much though I loved the Coral Island and the bower* which had now been our home so long, I felt that I could have quitted all at that moment without a sigh. With joyful anticipations we hastened to the highest point of rock near our dwelling, and awaited the arrival of the vessel, for we now perceived that she was making straight for the island, under a steady breeze.

In less than an hour she was close to the reef, where she rounded to, and backed her topsails* in order to survey the coast. Seeing this, and fearing that they might not perceive us, we all three waved pieces of cocoa-nut cloth in the air, and soon had the satisfaction of seeing them beginning to lower a boat and bustle about the decks as if they meant to land. Suddenly a flag was run up to the peak, a little cloud of white smoke rose from the schooner's side, and, before we could guess their intentions, a cannon-shot came crashing through the bushes, carried away several cocoa-nut trees in its passage, and burst in atoms against the cliff a few yards below the spot on which we stood.

* schooner — a type of ship   * bower — a shaded place under trees
* backed her topsails — turned some sails around to slow down the boat

Practice Questions — Fiction

With feelings of terror we now observed that the flag at the schooner's peak was black, with a Death's head and cross bones upon it. As we gazed at each other in blank amazement, the word "pirate" escaped our lips simultaneously.

"What is to be done?" cried Peterkin, as we observed a boat shoot from the vessel's side, and make for the entrance of the reef. "If they take us off the island, it will either be to throw us overboard for sport, or to make pirates of us."

I did not reply, but looked at Jack, as being our only resource in this emergency. He stood with folded arms, and his eyes fixed with a grave, anxious expression on the ground. "There is but one hope," said he, turning with a sad expression of countenance* to Peterkin; "perhaps, after all, we may not have to resort to it. If these villains are anxious to take us, they will soon overrun the whole island. But come, follow me."

Stopping abruptly in his speech, Jack bounded into the woods, and led us by a circuitous* route to Spouting Cliff. Here he halted, and, advancing cautiously to the rocks, glanced over their edge. We were soon by his side, and saw the boat, which was crowded with armed men, just touching the shore.

* expression of countenance — a facial expression
* circuitous — long and winding

1) In the first paragraph, why do the boys scramble up the rocks?

    ....

    ....

2) *"So it is, and a schooner, too!" said Jack, as he proceeded hastily to dress.* Which of the following best matches the meaning of the word *hastily* in the sentence above?

    Tick **one** box.

    angrily   [ ]

    gradually   [ ]

    thoughtfully   [ ]

    quickly   [ ]

Practice Questions — Fiction

3) The boys' hearts are *thrown into a terrible flutter* when they see the boat for the first time.
What does this description tell you about how the boys are feeling?

....

4) How can you tell that Ralph has mixed feelings about leaving the island?

....

5) Why does white smoke rise from the side of the boat?

....

6) Look at the paragraph beginning, *In less than an hour...*
Find and copy a word or phrase from this paragraph that suggests the cannonball has caused a lot of damage.

....

7) Why do the boys think the boat is a pirate ship?

....

8) Look at the paragraph beginning, *I did not reply.*
Explain how Jack's speech and actions in this paragraph show that he is a good leader.

....

....

....

Practice Questions — Fiction

9) Look at the paragraph beginning, *Stopping abruptly...*
Find and copy a word from the rest of the paragraph that
suggests Jack is being careful not to be seen by the pirates.

....

10) Using information from the text, tick one box in each
row to show whether each statement is true or false.

Statement	True	False
Jack is the first one to see the ship.		
Several hours pass between the ship being spotted and the ship approaching the reef.		
The boys are surprised to find out that the ship belongs to pirates.		
Peterkin is concerned about what might happen if the pirates find them.		
Jack is confident that his plan is going to work		

11) How do the boys' attitudes towards the boat change throughout the extract?

....

....

12) What do you think might happen to the boys next?
Use evidence from the last paragraph to support your prediction.

....

....

....

....

Practice Questions — Non-Fiction

Read this article about libraries, then answer the questions below.

Libraries

The word 'library' often conjures up images of *Harry Potter's* Hogwarts School or Victorian country houses: centuries-old buildings housing row upon row of bookcases, each buckling under the weight of the countless large, cobweb-laden tomes on their shelves. For some, libraries belong in a world of candles, cloaks and horse-drawn carriages.

But libraries in fact have a far richer history, stretching back to a time long before the Victorian era.

The first libraries date back to the ancient world. Archaeologists have found evidence suggesting that some ancient Egyptian towns had buildings which stored rolls of papyrus and parchment. By far the most renowned of these ancient libraries was the Great Library of Alexandria, which was established by a king called Ptolemy. Ptolemy set out to collect all of the books in the world, which he then stored in the library as papyrus scrolls. They were written in a range of different languages and transported from distant places, which took huge amounts of time and effort. At its height, the library is believed to have held over 700,000 scrolls of parchment — a huge feat.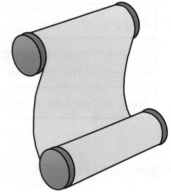

From Egypt, the idea of libraries soon spread across the world, including to Rome and eventually to the rest of Europe. By the 1800s, libraries as we know them had been founded in Britain, France, Italy, Spain and Germany. Universities, governments and other organisations paid large sums of money for ornate buildings to house their books.

Arguably the most significant moment in the history of British libraries came in 1850, when the government passed the Public Libraries Act, which allowed any local council to set up its own library. The new law was partly the work of Edward Edwards, a bricklayer who used a local college library to educate himself. The new law did face opposition from some politicians, who thought that the scheme was too costly, and a few rich people disliked the idea of giving poorer people access to books for free. But the law passed successfully — the first free public library in Britain was the Manchester Free Library, founded in 1852. Edward Edwards was its first librarian, and on its opening it held over 18,000 books.

Practice Questions — Non-Fiction

An important innovation for libraries was the Dewey Decimal System. It was invented in 1876 by an American librarian called Melvil Dewey while he was working at a university library in Massachusetts. The Dewey Decimal System uses numbers to classify library books by subject area, simplifying the process of organising and locating books in a large collection. It rapidly became the most popular way to organise library books and is still used today.

The Dewey Decimal System made Melvil Dewey a household name. Many other illustrious figures worked in libraries during their lifetimes, including authors such as Philip Pullman and Lewis Carroll, and the poet Philip Larkin. In fact, it was during Larkin's time as a librarian at the University of Hull that he wrote some of his most popular poems.

Unfortunately, the increasing popularity of the internet has contributed to a drop in library use over the past few years: around 10 million British people regularly use their public library today, compared to around 15 million ten years ago. With information available online at the click of a mouse and cheap books available to order over the internet, is it any wonder that libraries are finding it increasingly difficult to remain open?

Thankfully, many libraries have managed to adapt in order to maintain their place in the public consciousness. Libraries now host book festivals, music concerts and other events to entice new visitors. For example, in 2015, the Dokk1 library in Denmark was unveiled; it has a wealth of facilities, including art exhibitions, classrooms and playgrounds. It has already been very successful — the year after it opened, it was named public library of the year.

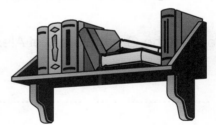

1)   What does *a far richer history* tell you about libraries?

Tick **one** box.

Libraries in the present are better than those in the past. ☐

Libraries have a more interesting and important history than people think. ☐

Libraries have a lot more money than people first thought. ☐

Libraries have grown too powerful and need to be stopped. ☐

Practice Questions — Non-Fiction

2) Look at the paragraph beginning, *The first libraries date back...*
   What does the word *renowned* tell you about the Great Library of Alexandria?

   ....

3) Why was the Great Library of Alexandria considered a *huge feat*? Give one reason.

   ....

4) Look at the paragraph beginning, *From Egypt...*
   What is the meaning of the word *ornate* in this paragraph?

   ....

5) Give two reasons why the Public Libraries Act had to *face opposition*.

   1. ....

   2. ....

6) How did the Great Library of Alexandria compare to the Manchester Free Library?

   ....

   ....

7) Why was the Dewey Decimal System an *important innovation*?

   ....

8) Find and copy a word or group of words that shows that
   the Dewey Decimal System made Melvil Dewey famous.

   ....

Practice Questions — Non-Fiction

9) According to the text, how did the rise of
    the internet lead to a decline in library use?

    ....

    ....

10) *Libraries now host book festivals, music concerts and
    other events to entice new visitors.*
    What does the word *entice* mean in the sentence above?

    ....

    ....

11) What do you think will happen to libraries in the future?

    ....

    ....

12) Below is a list of summaries of paragraphs from the text.
    Number them 1-6 in the order in which they appear in the text.

    There is still hope for libraries.

    Several famous people worked in libraries.

    A description of the first libraries.

    A new system to organise books is described.

    An explanation for the decline of library use.

    A description of the Public Libraries Act.

Practice Questions — Poetry

Read this poem, then answer the questions on the next page.

The Superstitious Ghost

I'm such a quiet little ghost,
Demure* and inoffensive;
The other spirits say I'm most
Absurdly apprehensive.

Through all the merry hours of night
I'm uniformly cheerful;
I love the dark, but in the light,
I own, I'm rather fearful.

Each dawn I cower down in bed,
In every brightness seeing
That weird, uncanny form of dread —
An awful Human Being!

Of course I'm told they can't exist,
That Nature would not let them;
But Willy Spook, the Humanist,
Declares that he has met them!

He says they do not glide like us,
But walk in eerie paces;
They're solid, not diaphanous,*
With arms! and legs! and faces!!!

They talk of 'art,' the horrid crew,
And things they call 'ambitions.'
Oh yes, I know as well as you
They're only superstitions.

And some are beggars, some are kings,
Some have and some are wanting;
They squander time in doing things
Instead of simply haunting.

But should the dreadful day arrive
When, starting up, I see one,
I'm sure 'twill scare me quite alive;
And then — oh, then I'll be one!

* demure — shy
* diaphanous — see-through

Arthur Guiterman

Practice Questions — Poetry

1) *I'm such a quiet little ghost...*
Find and copy two more words in the poem that make the ghost seem timid.

....

2) What does the superstitious ghost do during the daytime?

....

3) What is the superstitious ghost afraid of?

....

4) Give one difference between humans and ghosts, according to the poet.

....

5) *That weird, uncanny form of dread*
How does this phrase make the reader feel about human beings?

....

6) *He says they do not glide like us,*
But walk in eerie paces;
Which of the following is closest in meaning to the word *eerie* in this line?

Tick **one** box.

fearful ☐

strange ☐

unfamiliar ☐

realistic ☐

7) Look at the second half of the poem.
What do you think is one of the main ideas of this section of the poem?

....

Nouns

Nouns are words that name something. Here are some special types of noun to look out for.

Proper Nouns **Always Need a** Capital Letter

Proper nouns are names for particular people, places or things.
They always need a capital letter.

In July, Nabeel is going to Rome to see the Colosseum.

These are all examples of proper nouns.

Collective Nouns **Name a** Group **of Things**

Some nouns are special names for groups of things.
They include words like 'flock', 'crowd', 'pack' and 'swarm'.

The murder of crows flew past.

Emily watched the pride of lions hunt a herd of buffaloes.

Collective nouns are often names for groups of animals.

Abstract Nouns **are** Things **you can't** See

1) Some nouns name things you can't see, touch, taste,
smell or hear. These are called abstract nouns.

2) Abstract nouns are often ideas or emotions.

She has a lot of patience, and she's full of kindness.

- -
EXAMPLE:

Read the sentence below. Underline all of the nouns.

Luke felt a thrill as he watched the dolphins leaping into the air.

'Thrill' is an abstract noun — it's describing an emotion.
- -

"I can identify different types of noun."

Verbs

Verbs are useful words. They usually show an action that's being done by a person or thing.

The Subject and Verb Have to Agree

1) Verbs are <u>action</u> words. They <u>change</u> depending on <u>who</u> is doing the action.

> <u>We climb</u> up the mountain.   <u>Nadia climbs</u> down the ladder.

2) Whoever's <u>doing the verb</u> in a sentence is the <u>subject</u>. The <u>object</u> has the verb done <u>to it</u>.

> Passive sentences are a bit different. Have a look on p.35.

> <u>The cat</u> has stolen <u>my chair</u>.
> the <u>subject</u>   the <u>object</u>

Verbs Can Show How Likely Something is

1) These verbs are called <u>modal verbs</u>.

> Naomi <u>shall</u> bring her dog.
> '<u>Shall</u>' is the <u>modal verb</u>.

> could   should   might   must
> may   will   would   can

2) Some modal verbs can show how <u>likely</u> an action is.

These words usually show something is <u>less</u> likely.

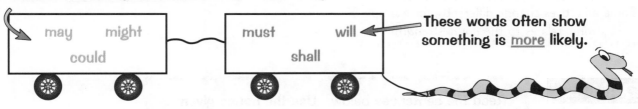

> may   might   could   must   will   shall

These words often show something is <u>more</u> likely.

EXAMPLE: Read the sentences below. Put a tick in each row of the table to show whether the modal verb shows <u>certainty</u> or <u>possibility</u>.

'Certainty' means something is <u>definite</u>.

'Possibility' means something is <u>unsure</u> or it might not happen.

Sentence	Certainty	Possibility
I may buy some books at the weekend.		✓
Kat must be upset that she lost the match.	✓	
She will help you with your homework.	✓	

"I can identify different types of noun and verb."

Adjectives

Adjectives are used to describe nouns. They can be used in different and wonderful ways.

Adjectives can go Before or After a Noun

Adjectives can be found in <u>different parts</u> of sentences.

> The <u>young</u> girls were very <u>happy</u>.

The adjective 'young' comes <u>before</u> the noun it describes — 'girls'.

Here, the adjective 'happy' comes <u>after</u> the noun.

Some Adjectives are Made From Other Words

Adjectives can sometimes be made from <u>verbs</u> or <u>nouns</u>. To do this you'll usually need to add an <u>ending</u> (a suffix) like '<u>ful</u>' or '<u>less</u>'.

pain ⟶ The graze on Tom's arm looks <u>painful</u>.

spot ⟶ The house was <u>spotless</u> after Charlie cleaned it.

'Spot' can be a <u>verb</u> or a <u>noun</u>.

There are <u>other endings</u> you might come across too: ⟶

expens<u>ive</u>   hero<u>ic</u>
danger<u>ous</u>   person<u>al</u>

> Some adjectives change differently, for example 'strong' relates to the noun 'strength'.

EXAMPLE:

> Read the sentences below. Use the nouns given in brackets to make <u>adjectives</u> that fill in the gaps.

Amelia thought that castles were ....<u>wonderful</u>.... (wonder). She was very ....<u>artistic</u>.... (artist), and she loved to paint old buildings. At the last castle she visited, she met an ....<u>adventurous</u>.... (adventure) knight.

You might have to <u>change</u> the <u>spelling</u> of a word before you add a suffix — see p.60.

"I know what adjectives are and how to make them from verbs or nouns."

 ✓ ✓   ✓

Section Two — Word Types

Adverbs

If you want to spice up the action you created with verbs, then adverbs will do the trick...

Adverbs Describe Verbs

1) Adverbs tell you <u>how</u>, <u>when</u>, <u>where</u> or <u>why</u> an action was done. Often, adverbs end in '<u>ly</u>'.

> Jamie poured the milk <u>clumsily</u>.

Watch out — some adjectives, like 'friendly' and 'lonely', end in 'ly' as well.

'<u>Clumsily</u>' tells you <u>how</u> the action was done.

> I'm going into town <u>tomorrow</u>, so I'll post your letter <u>then</u>.

'<u>Tomorrow</u>' and '<u>then</u>' tell you <u>when</u> actions are done.

2) Some adverbs, like '<u>maybe</u>', '<u>perhaps</u>' and '<u>probably</u>', show how <u>likely</u> something is.

> She'll <u>probably</u> win the race.

3) Sometimes, <u>a group of words</u> tells you more about an action. This is called an <u>adverbial</u>.

> The bananas walked <u>as fast as possible</u>.

> <u>A year ago</u>, I went on holiday to Spain.

An adverbial at the <u>start</u> of a sentence is called a <u>fronted adverbial</u>.

4) Some words can be an <u>adverb</u> or an <u>adjective</u>, depending on the sentence. For example, words like '<u>late</u>', '<u>hard</u>' and '<u>low</u>'.

> Stay <u>close</u> to the house!

'<u>Close</u>' is an <u>adverb</u> because it describes the verb '<u>stay</u>'.

> I'd prefer to go to a shop that's <u>close</u>.

'<u>Close</u>' is an <u>adjective</u> because it describes the noun '<u>shop</u>'.

Adverbs Also Describe Adjectives

Words like '<u>very</u>', '<u>quite</u>', '<u>extremely</u>' and '<u>nearly</u>' are <u>also</u> adverbs. They can be used with <u>adjectives</u> to show <u>how much</u> the adjective is working on the noun.

> The cake was <u>nearly</u> <u>finished</u>.

'<u>Nearly</u>' is an adverb working on the adjective '<u>finished</u>'.

Adverbs <u>always</u> come before the adjective they're describing.

> The children were <u>quite</u> <u>hungry</u>.

"I know what adverbs are and how to use them."

Prepositions

Prepositions are handy words that show where, when and why things happen...

Prepositions Can Tell You Where

1) <u>Prepositions</u> are words and phrases like '<u>under</u>', '<u>in front of</u>', '<u>between</u>' and '<u>with</u>'.

2) They tell you how <u>nouns</u> (or pronouns) are <u>related</u> to each other.

3) Some prepositions tell you <u>where</u> things are in relation to <u>other things</u> in the sentence.

> The dog carried the sausages <u>in</u> its mouth.

'<u>In</u>' tells you where the sausages are <u>in relation to</u> the mouth.

Prepositions Can Be About Time

Prepositions can also tell you <u>when</u> things happen in relation to <u>each other</u>.

> <u>Throughout</u> the year, there will be events celebrating their work.

> <u>In</u> summer, the girls play basketball <u>during</u> the week.

Some prepositions, like '<u>in</u>', can be used to talk about <u>when</u> or <u>where</u> something takes place.

EXAMPLE:

Underline the <u>prepositions</u> in this sentence.

<u>On</u> Mondays, the rhino runs <u>through</u> the fruit market.

'<u>On</u>' and '<u>through</u>' are the correct answers because they tell you <u>when</u> and <u>where</u> the rhino was in the fruit market.

Prepositions Can Explain Why Too

Some prepositions tell you <u>why</u> two things are <u>connected</u>.

> <u>As</u> a fan of kayaking, she frequently went to the lake.

'<u>As</u>' explains <u>why</u> she goes to the lake — <u>because</u> she loves kayaking.

> They had to cancel the funfair <u>because of</u> the weather.

"I know what prepositions are and how to use them."

Pronouns

Pronouns help to keep sentences interesting by avoiding the repetition of nouns.

Pronouns Replace Nouns

1) <u>Pronouns</u> save you from <u>repeating a noun</u> over and over again.

2) Pronouns like '<u>they</u>', '<u>we</u>' and '<u>him</u>' can <u>replace</u> nouns in a sentence.

> Leanne has always loved jam. <u>She</u> eats <u>it</u> every day.

These pronouns are used when the <u>person or thing</u> is <u>doing</u> the action.

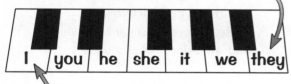

| I | you | he | she | it | we | they |

The pronoun 'I' always needs a <u>capital letter</u>.

Use these pronouns when the <u>person or thing</u> is having the action <u>done to it</u>.

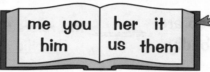

| me | you | her | it |
| him | | us | them |

3) It's important that a text makes sense — this is called '<u>cohesion</u>'. You need to make sure it's clear <u>who</u> you're <u>talking about</u>:

> Bhavesh asked Rob if <u>he</u> could play baseball.

It's <u>not clear</u> if the 'he' refers to Bhavesh or Rob.

Possessive Pronouns Show Belonging

Possessive pronouns tell you who <u>owns</u> something.

| mine | yours | his |
| hers | ours | theirs |

> This punching bag is <u>mine</u>. <u>Yours</u> is over there.

Relative Pronouns Point Back to Something

<u>Relative pronouns</u> are used to <u>add information</u> about something that's <u>already</u> been mentioned in a sentence. They include words like:

who   that
which   whose

> The man, <u>whose</u> jacket is torn, is standing beside the goat.

"I know what pronouns are and how to use them." ✓ ✓ ✓

Determiners

Determiners might sound scary, but don't panic — you already use them all the time.

Determiners Tell You More About Nouns

Determiners are <u>small words</u> that go before <u>nouns</u>.
They can show whether a noun is <u>specific</u> or <u>general</u>.

<u>That</u> cow gave him a fright. ✎➜ This means a <u>specific cow</u>.

These could be <u>any horses</u>. ✎➜ There were <u>some</u> horses in the field.

<u>These</u> sheep are behaving badly. ✎➜ This refers to <u>several specific sheep</u>.

> Articles ('a', 'an' and 'the') are another type of determiner. 'A' is used before consonant sounds and 'an' before vowel sounds.

They Show How Many Things There Are

<u>Determiners</u> can also tell you <u>how many</u> things there are.

<u>Five</u> bees chased the bear.

There are <u>several</u> pairs of socks under the bed.

Determiners Also Show Who Owns Something

Words like '<u>my</u>' and '<u>our</u>' explain who something <u>belongs</u> to.

Ronan wore <u>his</u> favourite suit to the interview.

Suki and Harry took <u>their</u> pet tortoise on holiday.

EXAMPLE:

Read the sentence below. Underline the <u>determiners</u>.

Janine decorated <u>every</u> cake with <u>some</u> icing in <u>her</u> favourite colour.

Remember that determiners can show whether something is <u>general</u> or <u>specific</u>.

"I know what determiners are and how to use them."

Practice Questions

1) Write your own sentence using the word '**handle**' as a **noun**. Use the correct punctuation in your sentence.

   ....

   Write your own sentence using the word '**handle**' as a **verb**. Use the correct punctuation in your sentence.

   ....

2) Read the sentences below and circle the **nouns**.

   The excitement of seeing a pod of whales made Starr jump for joy. She grabbed her camera and started to film.

3) Read the sentences below. Tick the event that is **least likely** to happen.

   Tick **one** box.

   There might be a thunderstorm tonight. ☐

   There will be a thunderstorm tonight. ☐

   There should be a thunderstorm tonight. ☐

   There shall be a thunderstorm tonight. ☐

4) Read the sentences below. Explain how the **modal verb** gives the second sentence a **different meaning**.

   Rosina and her brother play squash with their cousin.
   Rosina and her brother might play squash with their cousin.

   ....

   ....

Practice Questions

5) Look at the table below. Add a **suffix** to each noun to make it an adjective.

Noun	Adjective
power	
noise	
energy	
adventure	

6) Put a tick in each row of the table below to show whether the words in bold are **adjectives** or **adverbs**.

Sentence	Adjective	Adverb
My dad watches the news **daily**.		
Paulina's gran buys the **daily** newspaper.		
That meal you cooked us was **lovely**.		

7) Read the sentence below and underline the **adverbs**.

Her dress is quite ugly, so maybe she'll buy a different one tomorrow.

8) Rewrite the sentence below so it starts with the **adverbial**. Only use the words from the sentence, and make sure you use correct punctuation.

I had to go to an appointment before work.

....

Practice Questions

9) Read the sentences below. Choose a **preposition** from the box to fill each gap and write it on the line. You can only use each preposition **once**.

> | beside | because of | throughout |

Emil had to go to the doctor .... his sore knee.

Alison was eating sweets .... the exam.

The new post office is .... the butcher's.

10) Write down the correct **possessive pronoun** to replace the word or words that are underlined in each sentence.

That car belongs to Greg and Amy. That car is ....

Those roller skates belong to me. Those roller skates are ....

This picnic blanket is owned by us. This picnic blanket is ....

11) Read the sentences below and circle the **relative pronouns**.

The restaurant which Sanjay and Imogen like was recently given an award. It's the same award that the restaurant next door got last year.

12) Read the sentences below and circle the **determiners**.

I have to sew some buttons onto this jacket.
Isla has fifteen hens, but that hen is her favourite.

Sentences

Sentences have a few different jobs to do. Here's a page to help you get to grips with them...

Statements **Normally Provide** Information

Statements are sentences which <u>tell</u> you something.
The <u>words</u> in a statement are usually in the <u>same order</u>.

<u>Christine</u> opened <u>the door</u>.

The <u>subject</u> (the person or thing <u>doing</u> the verb) usually comes <u>first</u>.

The <u>object</u> usually comes after the verb. It's the person or thing that the verb is being <u>done to</u>.

Questions Ask **About Something**

Questions often start with a <u>question word</u>, but <u>statements</u> can also be turned into questions.

<u>Which</u> socks are yours?

<u>She is</u> absent. → <u>Is she</u> absent?

In <u>informal writing</u>, <u>question tags</u> are sometimes used:

He prefers to cycle to work, <u>doesn't he</u>?

The question tag '<u>doesn't he</u>' turns this statement into a <u>question</u>.

Give Instructions **or** Orders **with** Commands

Commands tell people <u>what to do</u>.

<u>Write</u> in pencil or black pen.

<u>Commands</u> can end in a <u>full stop</u> or an <u>exclamation mark</u>. Use an <u>exclamation mark</u> for <u>strong</u> or <u>urgent</u> commands.

These are the <u>verbs</u> that give the <u>order</u>.

<u>Don't touch</u> that vase!

Use Exclamations **to Show** Strong Feelings

Exclamations are used to show <u>strong emotions</u> like excitement, pain, surprise or anger.
They <u>always</u> start with '<u>what</u>' or '<u>how</u>', and they <u>must</u> contain a <u>verb</u>.

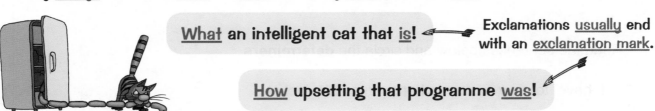

<u>What</u> an intelligent cat that <u>is</u>!

Exclamations <u>usually</u> end with an <u>exclamation mark</u>.

<u>How</u> upsetting that programme <u>was</u>!

"I can identify different types of sentence."   ✓ ✓ ✓

Clauses and Phrases

There's lots to learn about clauses and phrases — don't worry though, help is here.

Sentences are Built Around a Main Clause

1) A <u>clause</u> is part of a sentence which has a <u>subject</u> and a <u>verb</u>.

2) A <u>main clause</u> is a clause that would <u>make sense</u> as a <u>separate sentence</u>.

This is a <u>main clause</u>.

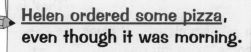

Helen ordered some pizza, even though it was morning.

Subordinate Clauses Add Information

Less important clauses are called <u>subordinate clauses</u> — they <u>add</u> <u>extra information</u> to the sentence.

I'm going to the shop <u>because there's no milk</u>.

Sometimes a subordinate clause can come <u>before</u> the <u>main clause</u>.

<u>Although it was quite long</u>, the talk was interesting.

You need a comma <u>after</u> the <u>subordinate clause</u>.

Subordinate Clauses Don't Make Sense Alone

There's an <u>easy</u> way to <u>tell</u> which clause is the <u>subordinate clause</u> in a sentence. <u>Main</u> clauses <u>make sense</u> on their <u>own</u>. <u>Subordinate</u> clauses <u>don't</u>.

<u>If she has time</u>, <u>Michelle goes running twice a day</u>.

'If she has time' <u>doesn't</u> make sense on its <u>own</u>. It's the <u>subordinate clause</u>.

'Michelle goes running twice a day' <u>makes</u> <u>sense</u> on its <u>own</u>. It's the <u>main clause</u>.

EXAMPLE:

Rewrite the sentence below by adding a <u>subordinate clause</u> to it. Make sure you use correct punctuation.

Anita wrote her essay upstairs.

Anita wrote her essay upstairs <u>because Lou was playing the guitar</u>.

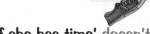 You could also add a subordinate clause at the start of the sentence, e.g. '<u>Since the lounge was being painted</u>'.

Remember it would need a <u>comma</u> after it.

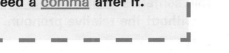

Clauses and Phrases

Relative Clauses Tell you More About Nouns

1) A relative clause is a type of subordinate clause that gives extra information about a noun.

Relative clauses usually start with:

> which   whose   where
>   when   who   that

This is a relative clause. It gives you some extra information about the noun — the uniform.

'That' is a relative pronoun (see p.25).

> The uniform that they wear to play baseball is grey.

EXAMPLE: Read the sentences below and underline the relative clause in each one.

> The hose that is bright orange isn't working.
>
> Our neighbour, whose name is Gerald, is quite deaf.
>
> That was the moment when I realised that I disliked peas.
>
> I bought my mum the perfume that she likes.

Look out for relative pronouns to help you identify relative clauses.

Sometimes the Relative Pronoun is Left Out

1) Sometimes you can leave out the relative pronoun from a sentence.

> I bought the salad that you asked for.

relative pronoun ✂

This is a relative clause that doesn't have a relative pronoun. ✂

> I bought the salad you asked for.

2) Sometimes you can't leave it out — the sentence won't make sense.

> The girl who has blue hair is my friend.

This sentence doesn't make sense without the relative pronoun.

> The girl has blue hair is my friend.

Clauses and Phrases

Phrases Normally Don't Have a Verb

A phrase is part of a sentence, usually without a verb.

1) A preposition phrase is a group of words which tell you when or where something or someone is.

You have an appointment on Friday at 3pm.

2) Preposition phrases always start with a preposition (see p.24).

The cups are in the box over there.

'In' is a preposition.

Noun Phrases Describe Things

A noun phrase is a group of words which includes a noun and any words that describe it.

My dad threw out the mouldy ham sandwich under my bed.

This uses an adjective ('mouldy'), a noun ('ham') and a preposition phrase ('under my bed') to expand the noun phrase.

EXAMPLE:

Read the sentence below. Underline the longest noun phrase there is in the sentence.

The lonely wizard with the purple hat wandered through the castle.

'Lonely' and 'with the purple hat' all describe the wizard, so they're part of the noun phrase.

Adverbial Phrases Work Like Adverbs

An adverbial phrase is a group of words that acts like an adverb. They can also be called adverbials. They can describe why, when, where and how often something happens.

Alyssa goes swimming three times a week.

Adverbials at the start of sentences are called fronted adverbials.

After work, Frank phoned me with the news.

"I can identify different clauses and phrases."

Conjunctions

Conjunctions are linking words — they join different parts of a sentence together.

Co-ordinating Conjunctions join Main Clauses

Co-ordinating conjunctions join two main clauses together to make one sentence.

> I didn't answer all the questions <u>for</u> there wasn't enough time.

'<u>For</u>' links the two main clauses <u>together</u>.

> Use <u>FANBOYS</u> to remember these seven <u>co-ordinating conjunctions</u>:
> <u>F</u>or <u>A</u>nd <u>N</u>or <u>B</u>ut <u>O</u>r <u>Y</u>et <u>S</u>o

Subordinating Conjunctions also join Clauses

You can join a <u>main clause</u> and a <u>subordinate clause</u> together using a <u>subordinating conjunction</u>. Here are some subordinating conjunctions:

> although   if   because
> while   until

> The donkey whistles <u>if</u> he is happy.

Subordinating conjunctions can go at the <u>start</u> of sentences as well as <u>between</u> two clauses.

> <u>Although</u> the cow was kicking, she managed to hold on.

Since the subordinate clause comes <u>first</u>, you need a <u>comma</u> here.

> See p.33 for more on preposition phrases.

EXAMPLE:

'<u>Before</u>' can be a <u>subordinating conjunction</u> or a <u>preposition</u>. Put a tick in each row to show which form '<u>before</u>' takes in each sentence.

Sentence	Preposition	Subordinating Conjunction
Ola tidies her room before school.	✓	
We got home before it started to rain.		✓

Here, 'before' is a <u>preposition</u>. It starts a preposition phrase.

'Before' is a <u>subordinating conjunction</u> here because it <u>links</u> the main clause to the subordinate clause.

"I can link ideas together using conjunctions."

Active and Passive

Active and passive sentences can be hard to spot. Here's a useful guide on how to do it.

Active Sentences Focus on Who

In <u>active</u> sentences, the <u>subject</u> does something <u>to</u> the <u>object</u>.

<u>Greg</u> is <u>doing</u> the action. He's the <u>subject</u>.

<u>Greg</u> plays with <u>the remote-controlled car</u> in the kitchen.

The <u>remote-controlled car</u> is the <u>object</u>. It's having the action done <u>to it</u>.

Passive Sentences Focus on What

When a sentence is in the <u>passive voice</u>, something is <u>done to</u> the subject.

<u>The tennis balls</u> were hit by Teresa.

the subject

<u>Gavin</u> was given the present.

You <u>don't</u> always need to say <u>who</u> does the action in passive sentences.

Gavin is the <u>subject</u> here.

<u>The exam</u> had <u>been</u> marked by a strict teacher.

the subject

You have to add '<u>been</u>' when writing the <u>past perfect</u> form in a <u>passive</u> sentence.

EXAMPLE:

Rewrite the sentence below so that it is in the <u>passive voice</u>. Use the words from the sentence, and add extra words where appropriate.

Percy owned the stack of books.

The stack of books <u>was owned by</u> Percy.

Watch out — the <u>subject</u> is 'the <u>stack</u> of books', not the books, so it must be '<u>was owned</u>', not 'were'.

"I can identify active and passive sentences and change the voice of sentences."

 ☑ ☑ ☑

Section Three — Sentences and Tenses

Tenses

This page might have you feeling a bit <u>tense</u> — grab a cup of tea to help this bit fly by.

The Tense Makes Verbs Change

1) Verbs <u>change</u> in different <u>tenses</u>, like the present tense and the past tense.

> I <u>throw</u> papers everywhere. ←——— simple present tense

2) You can often <u>add</u> '<u>ed</u>' to the verb to make it <u>simple past tense</u>, but some verbs <u>don't follow</u> this rule, for example:

> I <u>threw</u> papers everywhere.

> He <u>sang</u> me a song.

Present Perfect Tells you What's Happened

The <u>present perfect form</u> is used to talk about things that have <u>already happened</u>. It uses the <u>simple present tense</u> of 'have'.

> They <u>have</u> <u>fixed</u> the creaky door.

The door has <u>already</u> been fixed.

This verb is in the <u>present tense</u>.   This verb is in the <u>past tense</u>.

> Troy <u>has</u> <u>built</u> a treehouse in his garden.

The present perfect is a type of <u>present tense</u>.

> **EXAMPLE:**
>
> Read the passage below. Underline the verb form that is in the <u>present perfect</u>.
>
> My cousin is an excellent student. She got good marks at school and now she <u>has chosen</u> to go to university. She wants to be a scientist.
>
> The part after 'have' (or 'has') <u>isn't always</u> the same as the <u>simple past tense</u>.

Past Perfect Shows What Happened Before

The <u>past perfect form</u> tells you about something that happened <u>before</u> something else. It uses the past tense of 'have'.

By the time the shop opened, the door had <u>already</u> been fixed.

> They <u>had</u> <u>fixed</u> the creaky door when the shop opened.

The past perfect is a type of <u>past tense</u>.

> Ellie <u>had</u> <u>won</u> the race before we arrived.

Section Three — Sentences and Tenses

Tenses

Progressive Forms Use 'ing' Verbs

1) The <u>present progressive</u> form tells you that an action is <u>currently happening</u>. It uses the <u>simple present tense</u> of 'to be'.

She <u>is</u> <u>dancing</u> to her favourite songs.

'<u>Is</u>' is in the <u>present tense</u>. This means the 'ing' verb is <u>happening right now</u>.

2) If you want to say that something <u>was happening</u> in the <u>past</u>, you use the <u>past progressive</u> form. It uses the <u>simple past tense</u> of 'to be'.

She <u>was</u> <u>working</u> on her computer.

'<u>Was</u>' is in the <u>past tense</u>, so this means the action was happening <u>in the past</u>.

EXAMPLE: Complete the sentences below by filling in the gaps with the <u>past progressive</u> form of the verbs in the boxes.

| to lie |

My sister said she had put the rubbish out, but she ....<u>was lying</u>....

| to sit |

The bin bags ....<u>were sitting</u>.... by the front door. She came into

| to tell |

the kitchen when I ....<u>was telling</u>.... Dad, and he was very angry.

Tenses Need to be Consistent

It's <u>important</u> that tenses <u>match</u> in a piece of writing. If there's <u>no change in time</u>, verb tenses should <u>stay the same</u>. But, if the <u>time changes</u>, then the tense may also <u>change</u>.

Laurie decided to make himself a sandwich. He <u>takes</u> custard out of the fridge, put it on the bread and <u>adds</u> some ham.

These should be '<u>took</u>' and '<u>added</u>'.

"I can recognise and use different tenses."

Formal and Informal Writing

There are lots of differences between formal and informal writing — you need to know them.

Formal Texts Use Different Language

> Formal writing is used when writing to someone you <u>don't know</u> or someone you show <u>respect</u> to.

The words that formal texts use are often <u>more complicated</u> than the words in informal texts.

| The pasta smelled <u>yummy</u>. | ⟶ | The pasta smelled <u>delicious</u>. |

'Delicious' is more <u>formal</u>.

1) Informal writing might use <u>contracted forms</u> (see p.46) but formal writing <u>doesn't</u>.

Kay <u>won't</u> arrive on time. ⟶ Kay <u>will not</u> arrive on time.

↳ informal   ↳ formal

2) <u>Question tags</u> (see p.30) and <u>exclamation marks</u> aren't used in formal writing.

| You've got a horse, <u>haven't you</u>? | | <u>You've</u> got a horse! |

Formal Texts Might Use the Subjunctive Form

You might also see the <u>subjunctive form</u> in formal texts.

informal

| I hope that they <u>are</u> careful when they lift the piano. | I request that they <u>be</u> careful when lifting the piano. |
| It's important that he <u>gets</u> here as soon as he can. | It is important that he <u>get</u> here as soon as he can. |

subjunctive

Imaginary Situations Need the Subjunctive

The subjunctive can be used in sentences where the writer is talking about a situation that <u>isn't real</u>:

If I <u>was</u> older, I'd buy a boat. informal sentence

subjunctive form ⟵ If I <u>were</u> older, I would buy a boat.

> "I can recognise formal and informal language, including the subjunctive."

Standard and Non-Standard English

All your written work will be in Standard English, so it's important to write proper...ly.

The Subject and the Verb Must Agree

In Standard English, the verb has to agree with whoever's doing the action.

Amina and Theo <u>was</u> dancing. ⟶ **should be** ...<u>were</u> dancing.

Standard English is correct English.

Don't Mix up the Two Types of Past Tense

1) The <u>perfect form</u> of a verb is sometimes <u>different</u> to the <u>simple past tense</u> (see p.36).

<u>simple past tense</u>: I <u>swam</u> across the lake.   <u>perfect form</u>: I <u>had swum</u> across the lake.

2) <u>Don't mix up</u> the simple past tense and the perfect form.

I <u>swum</u> across the lake.

This is the verb form you use in the perfect form — it's <u>not</u> the <u>simple past tense</u>.

EXAMPLE: Read the sentence below. Underline the correct word in brackets to complete the sentence using <u>Standard English</u>.

Molly (<u>did</u> / done) lots of exercise today. ← 'Did' is <u>correct</u> in Standard English.

3) You usually need '<u>have</u>' or '<u>has</u>' with verbs like '<u>been</u>' or '<u>done</u>'.

I <u>seen</u> it. ⟶ **should be** I <u>have seen</u> it. OR I <u>saw</u> it.

non-Standard English

Don't get Confused by Pronouns

1) '<u>Them</u>' is a <u>pronoun</u> and '<u>those</u>' <u>points something out</u>. Don't mix them up.

<u>Them</u> penguins are scared. ⟶ **should be** <u>Those</u> penguins are scared.

A pronoun replaces a noun, so you can't have both 'them' (a pronoun) <u>and</u> 'penguins' (a noun) in this sentence.

2) <u>Don't</u> confuse '<u>that</u>' and '<u>what</u>' either. When you're talking about a noun that's <u>already</u> been <u>mentioned</u>, use '<u>that</u>'.

The joke <u>what</u> he told earlier. ⟶ **should be** The joke <u>that</u> he told earlier. ← noun

Section Three — Sentences and Tenses

Standard and Non-Standard English

Don't Forget the 'ly' at the End of Adverbs

Dropping the 'ly' from the end of an adverb is non-Standard English.

That dress fits you perfect. → should be → That dress fits you perfectly.

non-Standard English   Standard English

EXAMPLE:

Read the sentences below. Tick one box to show which sentence is written in Standard English.

The book was cleverly written. ☑

I drank the milk quick. ☐

My phone isn't working proper. ☐

Jason plays basketball brilliant. ☐

This is the only sentence where the 'ly' hasn't been missed out.

Avoid Double Negatives in Standard English

A double negative (writing two negatives in a sentence) is not usually Standard English.

I didn't buy nothing at the fair.

'Didn't' and 'nothing' are both negative words, which makes the sentence confusing.

I didn't buy anything at the fair.

I bought nothing at the fair.

These are both Standard English.

The negative word 'ain't' is non-Standard English. You need a word like 'isn't' or 'haven't' when using Standard English.

EXAMPLE: Read the sentence below. Underline the correct word in brackets to complete the sentence using Standard English.

Wendy didn't do (anything / nothing) that her gran asked her to.

'Anything' is correct in Standard English.

"I can recognise Standard and non-Standard English."

Section Three — Sentences and Tenses

Practice Questions

1) Read the sentence below and circle the word or words that make it a **question**.

"They're going to the museum today, aren't they?"

2) Rewrite the sentence below by adding a **subordinate clause** to it. Make sure you use correct punctuation.

Rory dropped the box of eggs.

....

....

3) Look at the table below. Add your own words before and after the noun to make your own **noun phrase**. One has already been done for you.

Noun	Noun phrase
the duck	the fluffy duck with white feathers
the pond	

4) Put a tick in each row of the table to show whether the conjunction in bold is a **co-ordinating conjunction** or **subordinating conjunction**.

Sentence	Co-ordinating conjunction	Subordinating conjunction
Coralie arrives next week **and** Dylan arrives the week after.		
I'll go to the shop **when** Dad finishes writing the list.		
The cat refused to drink the milk **because** it was cold.		

5) Rewrite the sentence below so it is in the **active voice**. Use the same words as the sentence and remove any words where appropriate. Use correct punctuation.

The model aeroplanes were built by Joseph and his grandpa.

....

....

Practice Questions

6) In the sentence below, the flight left before Sophie arrived.
    Read the sentence, then write the correct **verb** in the space.

    By the time Sophie arrived, the flight .... left.

7) Circle the two words that show the **tense** in the sentence below.

    I needed to repair the hole in my jumper, so my uncle taught me to sew.

8) Read the sentences below. Replace the words that are
    underlined with the correct words in the **past progressive form**.

    She <u>stared</u> through the open window.

    The hungry lioness <u>stalked</u> the antelope.

9) Read the sentences below. Underline the most **informal** sentence.

    Bethany thought the view was beautiful. Her brother wasn't
    too fussed. Bethany decided that she would return to the
    mountain whenever she could.

10) Read the sentence below. Replace the word in bold
    with a **more formal** word. Write the word in the box.

    Adam's schoolbag was so **messy** that he couldn't find anything in it.

Section Three — Sentences and Tenses

Practice Questions

11)   Read the sentences below. Tick the sentence which uses the **subjunctive form**.

Tick **one** box.

It is necessary that he sign the document. ☐

It is necessary for him to sign the document. ☐

It is necessary to sign the document. ☐

It is necessary when you sign the document. ☐

12)   Read the sentences below. Replace the words that are underlined with the correct words in **Standard English**.

The rabbit jumped around on the lawn <u>quick</u>.

You can exchange the CD for <u>them</u> DVDs on the table.

13)   Look at the table below. Put a tick in each row to show whether the sentence is in **Standard English** or **non-Standard English**.

Sentence	Standard English	Non-Standard English
Lisa swum smoothly through the water.		
You played that shot very beautiful.		
Zehra leapt gracefully over the large puddle.		
I don't have the time to finish all my work today.		

Punctuating Sentences

This stuff may seem easy, but make sure you know it inside out — you'll need it for the test.

Capital Letters Start Sentences

1) <u>Every sentence</u> has to <u>start</u> with a <u>capital letter</u>.

> **EXAMPLE:**
>
> Underline the words that need a capital letter.
>
> <u>the</u> school show was brilliant. <u>rafael</u> has a loud voice. <u>maybe</u> <u>i</u> will audition for a part next year.

<u>Proper nouns</u> (see p.20) and '<u>I</u>' always start with a <u>capital letter</u>, even when they're not at the beginning of a sentence.

2) To show where a sentence ends, you usually use a <u>full stop</u>.

Not All Sentences Finish with a Full Stop

There are <u>other ways</u> to finish sentences:

> The lion thought it would climb onto that car.
>
> There is a lion climbing onto my car!
>
> Why is there a lion climbing onto my car?

If the sentence shows <u>strong feelings</u>, like <u>surprise</u> or <u>anger</u>, replace the full stop with an <u>exclamation mark</u>.

Exclamation marks are usually used in speech or informal texts (see p.38).

If the sentence is asking something, it ends with a <u>question mark</u>.

Different Sentence Types Use Different Punctuation

1) <u>Statements</u> and <u>commands</u> usually end in <u>full stops</u>, but they can also end in <u>exclamation marks</u>.

> Pick up the weight, now!

This shows <u>strong feelings</u> so it gets an <u>exclamation mark</u>.

2) All <u>questions</u> <u>must</u> end with a <u>question mark</u>.

3) <u>Exclamations</u> nearly always end in <u>exclamation marks</u>.

"I can use capital letters, full stops, exclamation marks and question marks."

Commas

Commas are super handy punctuation marks — they often help to break information up.

Commas go Between Items in a List

When you use commas to <u>separate things</u> in a <u>list</u>, you don't put a comma between the <u>last two items</u>.

Put '<u>and</u>' or '<u>or</u>' between the last two items.

Rose bought a book, a box of chocolates, a candle <u>and</u> a CD for Cathy.

Put a <u>comma</u> after <u>each item</u> in the list except the last two.

This works for lists of <u>adjectives</u> too — as long as they're about the <u>same thing</u>.

Cathy thinks that Rose is kind, thoughtful <u>and</u> generous.

Commas Help you Add Extra Information

Commas are also used to join an <u>adverbial</u> to the front of a sentence:

Before going to the cinema, Tiziana chatted to Nathan.

fronted adverbial   comma

There's more about adverbials on page 33.

You Can Use Commas to Avoid Ambiguity

1) Some sentences can be <u>ambiguous</u> — this means that it's <u>not clear</u> exactly what the sentence is trying to say.

2) You can use <u>commas</u> to <u>avoid ambiguity</u> or <u>change the meaning</u> of a sentence.

Ants <u>which are very strong</u> can carry heavy objects.

This suggests that <u>only</u> very strong ants can carry heavy objects.

Ants, <u>which are very strong</u>, can carry heavy objects.

This tells you that <u>all</u> ants are very strong and can carry heavy objects.

EXAMPLE: Add a <u>comma</u> in the sentence below so that it is clear that <u>only</u> Miguel and Frankie dressed up as pirates.

After they left Charlie, Miguel and Frankie dressed up as pirates.

The comma here tells you that Miguel and Frankie dressed as pirates, but Charlie <u>didn't</u>.

"I can use commas to separate items in lists, after adverbials and to make sentences clearer."

Apostrophes

Apostrophes are great — they join two words together and can show who owns what.

Apostrophes **Join** Two Words **Together**

You can use an <u>apostrophe</u> to <u>join words together</u> and create a <u>new word</u> called a <u>contracted form</u>. These are only used in <u>informal writing</u>.

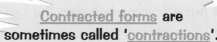

Contracted forms are sometimes called '<u>contractions</u>'.

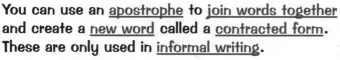

Let <u>us</u> → Let's

I <u>ha</u>ve → I've

I <u>wi</u>ll → I'll

Use an <u>apostrophe</u> to <u>replace</u> the <u>letters</u> that have been <u>missed out</u>.

We <u>will not</u> → We <u>won't</u>

Some <u>contracted forms</u> are a bit trickier, because they don't quite <u>match up</u> with the <u>missing letters</u> of the words they've <u>replaced</u>.

Apostrophes **Show** Possession

To show who owns something (<u>possession</u>), add an <u>apostrophe</u> and an '<u>s</u>' to the <u>owner's name</u>.

1) If there is only <u>one owner</u>, then add '<u>s</u>' to the <u>owner</u> or the <u>owner's name</u>.

The knight'<u>s</u> eyes turned red.

The princess'<u>s</u> horse was fast.

When a single owner <u>ends</u> in '<u>s</u>', you still need to add an apostrophe <u>and</u> an 's'.

2) If something <u>belongs</u> to a <u>group of people</u>, then follow these two rules.

The teachers<u>'</u> coffee machine was broken. → If the plural word <u>ends</u> in '<u>s</u>', <u>just</u> add an <u>apostrophe</u>.

Aida won the children<u>'s</u> technology competition. → If the plural word <u>doesn't</u> end in '<u>s</u>', add an <u>apostrophe</u> and an '<u>s</u>'.

EXAMPLE: Underline the word that includes an <u>apostrophe</u> for <u>possession</u>.

I would've missed my tennis lesson if I'd gone to <u>Jess's</u> party.

The party belongs to Jess. Her name ends in 's', but you still need to use an apostrophe <u>and</u> an 's'.

"I can use apostrophes to make contracted forms and to show possession."

Inverted Commas

For direct speech, inverted commas are the one piece of punctuation you always need.

Inverted Commas **Show** Direct Speech

1) Inverted commas go around direct speech — when you write down the exact words that someone says.

2) Always start direct speech with a capital letter and end it with a comma, full stop, exclamation mark or question mark.

3) Always put this punctuation inside the inverted commas.

> "Those shoes are too big," said Allie.

Inverted commas can also be called speech marks.

Punctuation **in Direct Speech** Varies

Punctuation in speech changes depending on how and where the sentence ends.

> "A moose just stole our map," said Zoe.

If the sentence carries on after the speech, put a comma (unless it's a question or it needs an exclamation mark).

> Niall shouted, "I know where I'm going!"

If the direct speech is at the end of the sentence, you need to add a comma after the clause that introduces it.

If the sentence ends when the speech ends, use a full stop, an exclamation mark or a question mark.

EXAMPLE:

Your friend has asked you to help them to punctuate this sentence correctly. Which two changes would you suggest?

> Amy yelled "Watch out for that log, Albert — don't trip over it."

The sentence ends with the speech, so you need a comma before the speech starts.

You need an exclamation mark because Amy is shouting an urgent command.

"I can punctuate speech correctly."

Colons, Semi-Colons and Dashes

It's easy to get confused about colons and semi-colons... These pages are here to help.

Colons Introduce Explanations

Colons show that you're about to <u>explain a point</u> you've <u>just made</u>. They normally <u>separate</u> two main clauses.

This bit should <u>make sense</u> on its <u>own</u>.

first point: more specific point

This is normally a <u>separate</u> <u>main clause</u>.

This is always about the <u>same thing</u> as the <u>first point</u>. It gives <u>more information</u> or an <u>explanation</u>.

EXAMPLE:

Add a <u>colon</u> to the sentence below so that it is punctuated correctly.

The detective was confused: <u>she had found some strange tracks that she couldn't explain</u>.

The <u>colon</u> goes <u>before</u> the explanation — it <u>separates</u> the explanation from the rest of the sentence.

Colons can also Introduce Lists

Colons can be used to show that a <u>list</u> is about to <u>begin</u>.

This <u>introduces</u> the <u>list of items</u>.

Only use a colon to introduce a list if it follows a <u>main clause</u>.

<u>There were five rooms in the witches' tower</u>: a cellar, a potion room, a library, a kitchen and a bedroom.

EXAMPLE:

Which sentence uses a colon correctly?

<u>The snowman took</u>: a broom, a bucket and some coal.

This is <u>incorrect</u>. This isn't a main clause, so you <u>don't need</u> a colon.

<u>The witch needs three things</u>: a hat, a wand and a cat.

This sentence is <u>correct</u>. A <u>main clause</u> introduces the list, so you need a colon.

Colons, Semi-Colons and Dashes

Semi-Colons Break up Lists

Semi-colons break up lists of long phrases or clauses (see p.31-33).

When I walked into the garden, the dog was fighting off a robber (who was raiding his kennel); my dad was water-skiing on the pond; and a goat, which was wearing a top hat, was leaning on the fence.

Some of these clauses **already** have commas or brackets in them.

Unlike with commas, you do need to put a semi-colon before the 'and' or 'or' that joins the last two things.

Semi-Colons and Dashes can Join Clauses

1) Semi-colons are used to join two related main clauses into one sentence. Both clauses must be about the same thing and equally important. They must also make sense on their own.

first clause

second clause

Lucius always takes guard duty seriously; Cato likes to shout silly jokes at Lucius.

EXAMPLE: Tick the sentence which uses a semi-colon correctly.

The second clause in this sentence doesn't make sense.

Dani likes to bake; every day Sendhil bakes on Fridays.

Dani likes to bake every day; Sendhil bakes on Fridays.   ✓

These clauses could be written as two separate sentences — the semi-colon joins them up.

2) A single dash can also join together two related main clauses.

The tree had been blown over — we couldn't get past.

"I can use colons, semi-colons and dashes correctly."

Adding Extra Information

Sentences sometimes have extra information — the punctuation used will show you where it is.

Brackets are Used to Separate a Parenthesis

1) A <u>parenthesis</u> is a part of a sentence that gives <u>extra</u> information.

2) <u>Brackets</u> go around a <u>parenthesis</u> and keep it <u>separate</u> from the rest of the sentence.

3) Brackets are <u>always</u> used in <u>pairs</u>.

> Amahle is the best player in the orchestra
> (<u>even better than her brother</u>).

This is the <u>parenthesis</u> — it adds some information, but you could <u>take it out</u> and the sentence would <u>still make sense</u>.

You Can Use Dashes and Commas too

1) A <u>pair of commas</u> can be used instead of brackets to separate a <u>parenthesis</u>.

> Malcolm, <u>the new chef at the hotel</u>, burnt the bacon.

This bit gives <u>extra information</u> about Malcolm — the <u>commas</u> go <u>either side</u> of it.

2) A <u>pair of dashes</u> can be used in the same way.

> Amanda — <u>the head chef</u> — wasn't happy with him.

This <u>parenthesis</u> explains who Amanda is, and it goes <u>between</u> the dashes.

EXAMPLE

Add <u>dashes</u> to the sentence so that it is correctly punctuated.

Nicholas — <u>who loves to read</u> — owns over 1000 books.

This is a <u>parenthesis</u> about Nicholas. It goes <u>inside</u> the dashes to separate it from the rest of the sentence.

> You can use a single dash to join two main clauses — see page 49.

"I can use brackets, dashes and commas to add a parenthesis."

Hyphens and Bullet Points

Hyphens and bullet points help to present information so that it isn't confusing.

Use Hyphens to Avoid Confusion

Hyphens can be used in phrases to show which word is being described. They help to avoid confusion.

> You can use hyphens to join words together or add prefixes (see p.59).

Could I have those two pound coins?

This means that the speaker is asking for two coins worth £1 each.

Could I have those two-pound coins?

Adding a hyphen shows that the words 'two' and 'pound' both describe the coins. Now, the sentence means that the speaker wants several coins worth £2.

EXAMPLE:

Add a hyphen to this sentence so it's clear the bird has big spots.

There was a big spotted woodpecker on the wall.

There was a big-spotted woodpecker on the wall.

The word 'big' describes the size of the bird's spots.

Bullet Points Break up Information

Bullet points are used in lists to separate different points.

> Grimm's School for Mythical Beings has three evening courses on offer:
> - A creative writing course
> - Mistress Cadaver's 'Biology of Mythical Beings' course
> - 'How to Make Friends with Humans'

A colon is used here to introduce the list of courses.

You can also put commas or semi-colons at the end of each bullet point, with a full stop after the final point.

If you use a capital letter at the start of one point, then use capitals at the start of all of the points.

"I can use hyphens and bullet points correctly."

Practice Questions

1) Read the sentence below. Insert the missing **comma** so that the sentence is punctuated correctly.

> Once she'd been to the gym the swimmer went home to have lunch with her parents.

2) Which sentence below uses **commas** correctly?

Tick **one** box.

Almost immediately the fire engine left, the station to attend the fire. ☐

After eating their lunch, the children went to play basketball in the playground. ☐

My brother's motorbike, car, and caravan are all being stored in my garage. ☐

In the kitchen the chefs were preparing, a large meal for the wedding guests. ☐

3) Karis's brother is called Andrew. Read the sentence below and add a **comma** to make the meaning clearer.

> Karis climbed a mountain with her brother, Andrew and the dog.

4) Circle the word below that uses an **apostrophe** for **possession**.

> I told my friends that I didn't want to go to the house that's on the hill (Lady Bowsprit lives there with her son's dogs), but they made me go there anyway. We went at nine o'clock after the sun went down.

5) Rewrite the sentences below so that they are punctuated correctly.

> "Don't go over there"! shouted Mabel. "there's a bear hiding behind that tree.

....

....

Practice Questions

6) Look at the table below. Put a tick in each row to show whether each sentence uses **colons** correctly or incorrectly.

Sentence	Correct	Incorrect
My half-sister is excellent: at running she trains for two hours each evening.		
Zaire loves broccoli he puts it in every meal: that he cooks for his family.		
We ran out: of milk my dad went to the shop to buy some milk and bread.		
The blackbird sat on the garden table: she was waiting for David to throw some raisins to her.		

7) Insert **colons** and **semi-colons** to the sentence below so it is punctuated correctly.

I found three rooms in the castle the kitchen (which had seven ovens) was on the ground floor the library was on the first floor and the master bedroom was at the top of the highest tower.

8) Read the sentence below. Insert a pair of **brackets** in the correct place.

When he travelled to the rainforest which was in Peru , Mr Riddle learned lots about the animals that lived there .

9) Which of these sentences is punctuated correctly?

Tick **one** box.

The three-storey building up the street nearly collapsed last-night. ☐

The three storey building up-the-street nearly collapsed last night. ☐

The three-storey building up the street nearly collapsed last night. ☐

10) Read the sentence below. Add a **hyphen** between two of the words, so that the meaning of the sentence changes.

The fast talking donkey managed to get himself out of trouble.

Prefixes

Prefixes are important — they get put in front of words and can change the meaning.

Prefixes **Go at the** Beginning **of a** Word

A <u>prefix</u> is a <u>letter</u> or <u>group</u> of letters added to the <u>beginning of a word</u> to form a <u>new word</u>.

$$\boxed{\underline{in}} \; + \; \boxed{secure} \; = \; \boxed{\underline{in}secure}$$

The prefix '<u>in</u>' is added to the word '<u>secure</u>' to make '<u>insecure</u>'.

The prefix '<u>re</u>' is added to the word '<u>turn</u>' to make '<u>return</u>'.

$$\boxed{\underline{re}} \; + \; \boxed{turn} \; = \; \boxed{\underline{re}turn}$$

Prefixes Can Change **the Word's** Meaning

Some <u>prefixes</u> can make a word have the <u>opposite meaning</u>.
E.g. '<u>un</u>' makes <u>verbs</u> and <u>adjectives</u> have the <u>opposite</u> meaning:

pack ⟶ <u>un</u>pack   kind ⟶ <u>un</u>kind

> When you add a prefix, the spelling of the root word doesn't change.

Adding a <u>prefix</u> like '<u>super</u>', '<u>anti</u>' and '<u>auto</u>' gives <u>nouns</u> a <u>new meaning</u>.

biography  <u>auto</u>biography

The prefix '<u>auto</u>' means <u>self</u>, so an '<u>autobiography</u>' is a biography you write about <u>yourself</u>.

Adding '<u>dis</u>', '<u>de</u>', '<u>mis</u>', '<u>over</u>' or '<u>re</u>' changes the meaning of <u>verbs</u>:

understand ⟶ <u>mis</u>understand

The prefix '<u>mis</u>' means <u>wrongly</u>, so '<u>misunderstand</u>' means to <u>understand incorrectly</u>.

EXAMPLE:

Explain how the different <u>prefixes</u> in the two sentences below change the word meanings.

The house was <u>unbuilt</u>.
This means that the house was ...<u>not built</u>...

The prefix '<u>un</u>' means '<u>not</u>', so '<u>unbuilt</u>' means '<u>not built</u>'.

The house was <u>rebuilt</u>.
This meant that the house was ...<u>built again</u>...

The prefix '<u>re</u>' means '<u>again</u>', so '<u>rebuilt</u>' means '<u>built again</u>'.

"I know what prefixes are and how they change the meaning of a word."

Suffixes

Suffixes are at the end of more words than you might think. This page shows how they work.

Suffixes Go at the End of a Word

1) A <u>suffix</u> is a <u>letter</u> or a <u>group</u> of letters that goes at the <u>end of a word</u> to form a <u>new word</u>.

lead	+	er	=	lead<u>er</u>
word		suffix		new word

The <u>suffix</u> is added to the <u>end</u> of the word '<u>lead</u>'.

2) Sometimes the <u>spelling changes</u> when a <u>suffix</u> is added.

Suffixes Can Be Added to Nouns

1) Add '<u>s</u>' or '<u>es</u>' to make a singular noun <u>plural</u>. → The <u>ducks</u> swam away.   I packed the <u>boxes</u>.

2) Add a <u>suffix</u> to an <u>adjective</u> or <u>verb</u> to make it a <u>noun</u>. The suffixes '<u>ment</u>', '<u>ness</u>', '<u>er</u>' and '<u>ity</u>' all form nouns.

teach<u>er</u> — '<u>Teach</u>' is a <u>verb</u>. '<u>Teacher</u>' is a <u>noun</u>.

agil<u>ity</u> — '<u>Agile</u>' is an <u>adjective</u>. '<u>Agility</u>' is a <u>noun</u>.

fair<u>ness</u> — '<u>Fair</u>' is an <u>adjective</u>. '<u>Fairness</u>' is a <u>noun</u>.

improve<u>ment</u> — '<u>Improve</u>' is a verb. '<u>Improvement</u>' is a noun.

Suffixes Can Form Verbs and Adjectives

Add suffixes like '<u>ate</u>', '<u>ise</u>' or '<u>ify</u>' to the end of a <u>noun</u> or <u>adjective</u> to make a <u>verb</u>:

energ<u>ise</u> — If you give someone <u>energy</u>, you '<u>energise</u>' them.

intens<u>ify</u> — If you make something more <u>intense</u>, you '<u>intensify</u>' it.

EXAMPLE:

Underline two suffixes which can be added to '<u>entertain</u>' to create new words.

<u>ment</u>   ise   ify   <u>er</u>   ness

Adding the suffix '<u>ment</u>' makes '<u>entertainment</u>'.

Adding the suffix '<u>er</u>' makes '<u>entertainer</u>'.

"I know what suffixes are and how they change the meaning of a word."

Word Families

Strange as it might seem, words have families. Words in the same family have the same <u>root</u>.

Word Families Come From the Same Root

1) Words in the same <u>word family</u> look like each other.
The bit of each word that is the <u>same</u> is called the <u>root</u>.

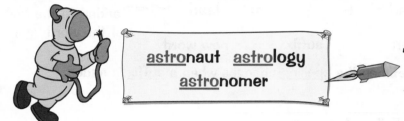

<u>astro</u>naut <u>astro</u>logy
<u>astro</u>nomer

All of these words have '<u>astro</u>' as their <u>root</u>, which means something that's to do with <u>stars</u> or <u>space</u>.

2) The root can be <u>anywhere</u> in the word — usually at the <u>beginning</u> or the <u>end</u>.

<u>dict</u>ionary   contra<u>dict</u>   re<u>flect</u>   <u>flex</u>ible

These words are in the same <u>word family</u> — they both have '<u>dict</u>' (meaning '<u>speak</u>') as their <u>root</u>.

Sometimes roots are <u>spelt</u> <u>slightly differently</u> in each word. The root means '<u>bend</u>' in both of these words.

Word Families Have Similar Meanings

Words in the same <u>word family</u> always have similar meanings. If you <u>don't know</u> what a root <u>means</u> straight away, see if you can <u>work it out</u> from the meanings of the words.

<u>mot</u>ion   pro<u>mot</u>e   <u>mot</u>orist

The root '<u>mot</u>' is to do with <u>things moving</u>.

The root '<u>memor</u>' is about <u>remembering things</u>.

<u>memor</u>y   com<u>memor</u>ate   <u>memor</u>ial

<u>col</u>lect   <u>col</u>league   <u>col</u>lision

You can make a good <u>guess</u> at the meaning of the root '<u>col</u>'. All of these words are about things <u>coming together</u>.

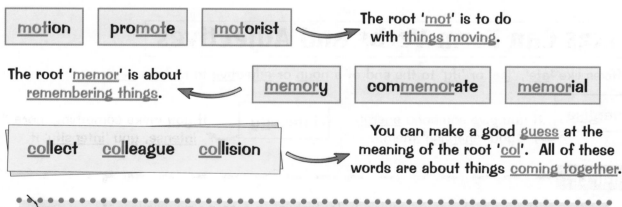

EXAMPLE: Underline the words in the same word family as '<u>liberty</u>'.

<u>liberal</u>   library   <u>liberator</u>
<u>liberate</u>   deliberate

'<u>Liber</u>' means <u>free</u>. Each underlined word is about <u>being free</u>.

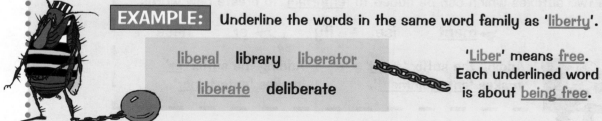

"I can tell which words are from the same family and work out what roots mean."

Section Five — Vocabulary

Synonyms and Antonyms

Synonyms and antonyms can be easily confused. Read this page carefully to avoid that.

Synonyms Mean the Same Thing

> A <u>synonym</u> is a word that has <u>the same</u> or
> a <u>very similar</u> meaning to another word.

Mick wasn't <u>scared</u> about the big dive.

frightened	anxious	nervous

These <u>synonyms</u> could <u>replace</u> the word '<u>scared</u>' and the sentence would have <u>the same</u> meaning.

EXAMPLE: Tick one word that is a synonym of '<u>mouldy</u>'.

stale ☐   rotten ✓   fresh ☐

'<u>Rotten</u>' means the same as '<u>mouldy</u>'.

Antonyms Are Opposites

An <u>antonym</u> is a word that means the <u>opposite</u> of another word.

Claire was a skunk with a <u>pleasant</u> smell.

repulsive	revolting	foul

These <u>antonyms</u> have the opposite meaning to '<u>pleasant</u>'.

EXAMPLE:

a) Give an explanation of the word <u>antonym</u>.

   An antonym is a word that's the opposite of another word.

b) Give one word that is an antonym of the word '<u>spicy</u>'.

   bland

"I know what synonyms and antonyms
are and can come up with my own." ☑ ☑ ☑

Section Five — Vocabulary

Practice Questions

1) **Explain how the different prefixes in the sentences below change their meanings.**

   The two wires in the computer were <u>disconnected</u>.

   This means that the two wires were ....

   ....

   The two wires in the computer were <u>reconnected</u>.

   This means that the two wires were..

   ....

2) **Circle two suffixes which can be added to the word below to create new words.**

   public   er   ify   ity   ise   ment

3) **Write down a word that belongs to the same word family as the words below.**

   recycle   cyclone   motorcycle   ....

4) a) **Give an explanation of the word synonym.**

   ....

   ....

   b) **Give one word that is a synonym of <u>jealous</u>.**

   ....

5) **Look at the table below. Complete the table by adding suitable antonyms.**

Word	Antonym
relaxed	
arrogant	

Prefixes

Prefixes don't usually change the spelling of a word, but they often change the meaning.

Prefixes Add Letters to the Front of Words

1) The original word <u>never changes</u> when a <u>prefix</u> is added, so <u>don't add</u> or <u>remove</u> letters.

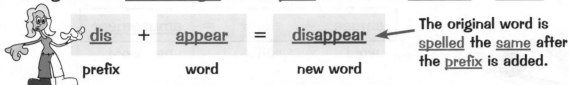

<u>dis</u> + <u>appear</u> = <u>disappear</u>

prefix   word   new word

The original word is <u>spelled</u> the <u>same</u> after the <u>prefix</u> is added.

2) If the prefix <u>ends</u> with the same <u>vowel</u> that the word <u>starts</u> with, add a <u>hyphen</u> between the prefix and the word.

<u>re</u>-<u>e</u>xamine   <u>co</u>-<u>o</u>wner

3) Some prefixes need a hyphen <u>whatever word</u> they're added to.

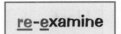

SELF-   <u>self</u>-belief   <u>self</u>-made   **EX-**   <u>ex</u>-wife   <u>ex</u>-mayor

4) Here are some <u>common</u> prefixes to learn:

<u>auto</u>graph	<u>sub</u>marine	<u>re</u>new
<u>super</u>hero	<u>anti</u>biotic	<u>inter</u>national

The Prefix 'in' Sometimes Changes Spelling

You can usually say that something is <u>not</u> something by adding the prefix '<u>in</u>'.

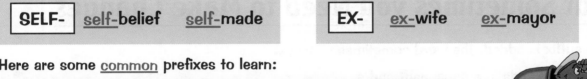

in + correct = <u>in</u>correct

'<u>Incorrect</u>' means '<u>not correct</u>'.

Be careful though — the prefix you need sometimes <u>changes</u> depending on the <u>word</u>.

1) If the <u>word</u> starts with '<u>l</u>', use '<u>il</u>':

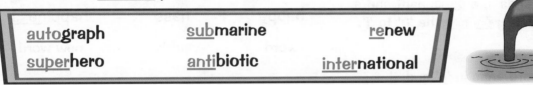

<u>il</u>legal   <u>il</u>legible   <u>il</u>logical

These words all have a <u>double 'l'</u>.

2) If the word starts with '<u>m</u>' or '<u>p</u>', use '<u>im</u>':

<u>im</u>mortal   <u>im</u>possible   <u>im</u>perfect

3) If the word starts with '<u>r</u>', use '<u>ir</u>':

<u>ir</u>regular   <u>ir</u>relevant   <u>ir</u>responsible

These words all have a <u>double 'r'</u>.

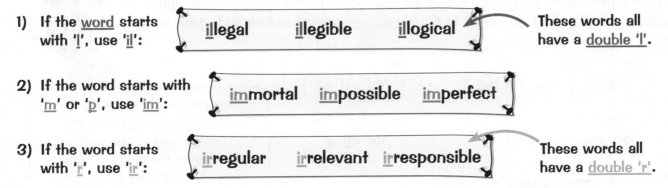

"I can spell words that have prefixes."

Suffixes and Word Endings

There's lots to remember about suffixes — here are some pages to help you get started.

Sometimes you can Add a Suffix Directly...

Often you can <u>add</u> a suffix <u>without</u> having to <u>change</u> the original word.

amuse	+	ment	=	<u>amusement</u>
word		suffix		new word

Suffixes can also make words <u>plural</u>:

blast + s = <u>blasts</u>   box + es = <u>boxes</u>

... But Sometimes you Need to Make Changes

When a suffix is added, the word sometimes <u>changes</u>.

1) If the word ends in a <u>consonant</u> and a '<u>y</u>', you normally <u>change</u> the '<u>y</u>' to '<u>i</u>'.

happy + ness = happ<u>i</u>ness
word   suffix   new word

2) When the word ends in '<u>e</u>' and the <u>first letter</u> of the <u>suffix</u> is a <u>vowel</u>, you lose the '<u>e</u>'...

sens<u>e</u> + ible = sens<u>i</u>ble
word   suffix   new word

3) ...unless the word ends in '<u>ge</u>' or '<u>ce</u>'.

mana<u>ge</u> + able = mana<u>ge</u>able
word   suffix   new word

Some Suffixes Need a Double Letter

If the suffix starts with a <u>vowel</u> and the word ends with a <u>vowel</u> followed by a <u>consonant</u> (e.g. 'in') you need to <u>double the consonant</u> before adding the suffix.

word   suffix   new word

regr<u>et</u> + <u>ing</u> = regre<u>tting</u>

perm<u>it</u> + <u>ed</u> = perm<u>itted</u>

Say the words <u>out loud</u> — if you <u>emphasise</u> the <u>last syllable before</u> the suffix it follows the <u>rule</u>. If you don't then it's an <u>exception</u>.

There are some <u>exceptions</u>, though:

condit<u>ion</u> + <u>er</u> = condition<u>er</u>   defe<u>at</u> + <u>ed</u> = defeat<u>ed</u>

Suffixes and Word Endings

'ent' and 'ant' Endings Can Sound the Same

Words that end in '<u>ent</u>' can sound similar to words ending in '<u>ant</u>'.
Follow these rules to know <u>which one to use</u> when you're spelling them:

1) Most '<u>ent</u>' <u>words</u> have a '<u>c</u>', '<u>qu</u>', '<u>d</u>' or '<u>g</u>' right before the 'ent'.

confi<u>dent</u>   de<u>cent</u>   fre<u>quent</u>   intelli<u>gent</u>

This rule <u>only works</u> when the 'g' makes a '<u>j</u>' <u>sound</u> — it's pung<u>ent</u> but eleg<u>ant</u>.

2) Otherwise, chances are it's an '<u>ant</u>' word.

assist<u>ant</u>   toler<u>ant</u>   expect<u>ant</u>   observ<u>ant</u>

3) These rules also work for words ending in '<u>ence</u>'/'<u>ency</u>' or '<u>ance</u>'/'<u>ancy</u>'.

emerg<u>ency</u>   accept<u>ance</u>
independ<u>ence</u>   pregn<u>ancy</u>

'able' and 'ible' Suffixes Are Different

The root is what's left after any prefixes or suffixes have been removed.

Learn these rules for '<u>ible</u>' and '<u>able</u>':

1) When the root is a <u>whole word</u>, you usually add the suffix '<u>able</u>'.

   Even if the root <u>ends</u> in '<u>ce</u>' or '<u>ge</u>', the spelling of the root word <u>doesn't change</u>. charge<u>able</u>   favour<u>able</u>

2) If you can add '<u>ation</u>' to the root, you usually need '<u>able</u>', not '<u>ible</u>'. E.g. '<u>consideration</u>' becomes '<u>considerable</u>'.

3) When the root is <u>not</u> a whole word, you add the suffix '<u>ible</u>'.

   poss   +   ible   =   poss<u>ible</u>

The 'ly' Suffix is Different for Some Words

The suffix '<u>ly</u>' turns an <u>adjective</u> into an <u>adverb</u> (see p.23).

ordinary ⟹ ordinari<u>ly</u>   simp<u>le</u> ⟹ simp<u>ly</u>   medi<u>c</u> ⟹ medic<u>ally</u>

If the word <u>ends</u> in '<u>y</u>', you usually <u>remove</u> the 'y' and add the suffix '<u>ily</u>'.

If the word <u>ends</u> in '<u>le</u>', the 'le' often changes to become '<u>ly</u>'.

If the word <u>ends</u> in '<u>ic</u>', you add '<u>ally</u>' onto the end.

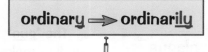
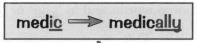

Section Six — Spelling

Suffixes and Word Endings

Adding Suffixes to 'fer' Endings Is Tricky

If you have to add a suffix to a '<u>fer</u>' ending, imagine saying it out loud. If the 'fer' is emphasised, add an '<u>r</u>' before the suffix. If it isn't then <u>just add the suffix</u>.

pre<u>fer</u> ⟶ pre<u>ferr</u>ed

'Fer' is <u>emphasised</u> here.

<u>differ</u> ⟶ <u>differ</u>ence

'Fer' <u>isn't</u> emphasised here.

'ous' Can Turn a Noun Into an Adjective

The suffix '<u>ous</u>' is often used to turn a noun into an <u>adjective</u>.

1) Sometimes you can just add '<u>ous</u>' onto the <u>end</u> of the <u>root</u> without changing the spelling, but sometimes the spelling of the root changes.

2) If the root ends in '<u>our</u>', you need to change the spelling before adding '<u>ous</u>':

glam<u>our</u> ⟶ glam<u>or</u>ous

The '<u>our</u>' in 'glamour' changes to '<u>or</u>'.

3) You have to <u>keep</u> the '<u>e</u>' in words that end with a '<u>j</u>' sound spelt '<u>ge</u>':   courag<u>eous</u>

4) Words that <u>sound like</u> 'ser<u>i</u>ous' usually have an '<u>i</u>' before the '<u>ous</u>' but sometimes have an '<u>e</u>':

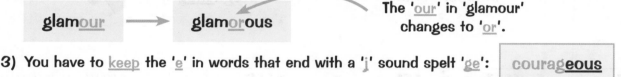

| ser<u>i</u>ous | var<u>i</u>ous | hid<u>e</u>ous | erron<u>e</u>ous |
| cur<u>i</u>ous | obv<u>i</u>ous | gas<u>e</u>ous | beaut<u>e</u>ous |

'sure' and 'ture' Sound Similar but Are Different

Words that sound like '<u>treasure</u>' are <u>spelt differently</u> to words that sound like '<u>picture</u>'.

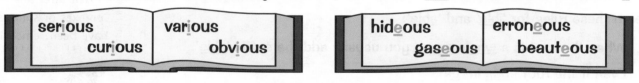

expo<u>sure</u>   lei<u>sure</u>

These words sound like '<u>treasure</u>'.

mix<u>ture</u>   lec<u>ture</u>

These words sound like '<u>picture</u>'.

Be Careful with 'que' and 'gue' Endings

Some words end in '<u>gue</u>' or '<u>que</u>' — you need to learn these.

The '<u>que</u>' ending makes a '<u>k</u>' sound.

pla<u>que</u>   uni<u>que</u>
mos<u>que</u>   opa<u>que</u>

lea<u>gue</u>   pla<u>gue</u>
ton<u>gue</u>   ro<u>gue</u>

The '<u>gue</u>' ending makes a '<u>g</u>' sound.

Suffixes and Word Endings

'cial' and 'tial' Make a 'shul' Sound

1) To find out whether you need 'cial' or 'tial', look at the letter that comes before it.

If it's a vowel, use 'cial'. ➞ artificial   social   crucial

residential   potential   presidential ⟵ If it's a consonant, use 'tial'.

2) But there are exceptions: 'financial', 'commercial' and 'initial' all break these rules.

Some Suffixes Sound Similar

Suffixes that sound like 'shun' are likely to be either 'tion', 'sion', 'ssion' or 'cian'.

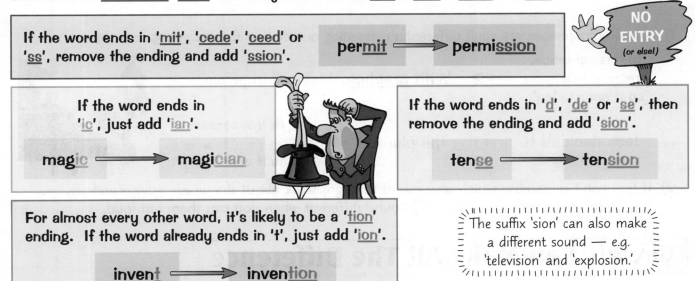

If the word ends in 'mit', 'cede', 'ceed' or 'ss', remove the ending and add 'ssion'.

permit ➞ permission

If the word ends in 'ic', just add 'ian'.

magic ➞ magician

If the word ends in 'd', 'de' or 'se', then remove the ending and add 'sion'.

tense ➞ tension

For almost every other word, it's likely to be a 'tion' ending. If the word already ends in 't', just add 'ion'.

invent ➞ invention

The suffix 'sion' can also make a different sound — e.g. 'television' and 'explosion.'

If a verb changes into a noun, you sometimes need to add 'ation'.
So the word 'confirm' would become 'confirmation'.

There's a Trick For 'tious' and 'cious' Suffixes

1) Some words end in a 'shuss' sound. These endings can be spelled 'tious' or 'cious'.

2) If a 'shun' suffix can be added to the word, then the 'shuss' is spelled 'tious'.

infection ⟵ infect ➞ infectious

3) Otherwise, 'shuss' is spelled 'cious'.   space ➞ spacious

"I can spell words with suffixes and other endings."

Homophones

A pair of pears might sound confusing — this page will help you to tell homophones apart.

Homophones Are Words that Sound the Same

A <u>homophone</u> is a word that <u>sounds the same</u> as <u>another word</u>, but has a <u>different meaning</u>.

I wrote the first <u>draft</u> of a story today. ← 'Draft' and 'draught' <u>sound the same</u> when they're said out loud, but they have <u>different meanings</u> and different <u>spellings</u>.

There's a <u>draught</u> coming from the window. ↙

1) Some homophones are spelt differently depending on whether they're <u>nouns</u> or <u>verbs</u>.

In this sentence, '<u>practice</u>' is a <u>noun</u>, → With <u>practice</u>, Jess will improve.
so it ends in '<u>ce</u>'.

In this sentence, '<u>practise</u>' is a <u>verb</u>,
so it ends in '<u>se</u>'.

Jess decided to <u>practise</u> the piano. ←

2) If you can't remember which way round they go, think about the words <u>advice</u> and <u>advise</u>. <u>Advice</u> (a <u>noun</u>) and <u>advise</u> (a <u>verb</u>) sound different when you say them out loud.

Vowels Can Make All The Difference

Sometimes words <u>sound the same</u> but have <u>different vowels</u>.

Cars on the road were <u>stationary</u>. | OR | I bought a lot of <u>stationery</u>.

'Station<u>a</u>ry' means 'not moving'. ↗

'Station<u>e</u>ry' is all the things you might find in your pencil case. ↗

Jo <u>complimented</u> Mo. | OR | My socks <u>complemented</u> my shoes.

'Compl<u>i</u>ment' means 'to say nice things about'. ↖

'Compl<u>e</u>ment' means 'to go well with'. ↗

The spell would <u>affect</u> Harriet most. | OR | The spell had an <u>effect</u> on Harriet.

'<u>A</u>ffect' is a verb. Remember: <u>a</u>ffect = <u>a</u>ction. ↗

'<u>E</u>ffect' is a noun. ↗

"I can spell different homophones." ✓ ✓ ✓

Section Six — Spelling

Silent and Unstressed Letters

You may not hear silent and unstressed letters, but it's important to be able to spot them.

Letters 'k', 'g' and 'w' Can Be Silent

1) Some words that sound like they start with '<u>n</u>' actually have a silent '<u>k</u>' or '<u>g</u>' at the start.

<u>k</u>nee <u>k</u>night

<u>w</u>rite <u>w</u>rong <u>g</u>naw <u>g</u>nome

<u>w</u>rist

2) Other words sound like they start with '<u>r</u>' but in fact have a silent '<u>w</u>' at the beginning.

There Are Many Other Silent Letters

Some words have a <u>silent 'b'</u>, often <u>after</u> the letter '<u>m</u>' or <u>before</u> the letter '<u>t</u>'.

plum<u>b</u>er lam<u>b</u> dou<u>b</u>t de<u>b</u>t

ta<u>l</u>k ha<u>l</u>f ca<u>l</u>m wa<u>l</u>k

There is a <u>silent 'l'</u> before the final '<u>k</u>', '<u>m</u>' or '<u>f</u>' in some words.

Some words that sound like they end in '<u>m</u>' have a <u>silent 'n'</u> at the end:

solem<u>n</u> colum<u>n</u> autum<u>n</u>

lis<u>t</u>en this<u>t</u>le fas<u>t</u>en

Sometimes there's a <u>silent 't'</u> after the letter '<u>s</u>'.

Unstressed Vowels Aren't Always Clear

<u>Sometimes</u>, vowels in a word sound like a <u>different vowel</u>. Other times, they sound like they're not there <u>at all</u>.

You don't hear the '<u>e</u>'.

origin<u>a</u>l sounds like origin<u>u</u>l

int<u>e</u>resting sounds like intresting

Look out for the <u>unstressed vowels</u> in these words:

sep<u>a</u>rate cal<u>e</u>nd<u>a</u>r bus<u>i</u>ness

diff<u>e</u>rent defin<u>i</u>te acc<u>o</u>mp<u>a</u>ny

"I can spell words with silent and unstressed letters."

66

Spelling Tricky Words

Some words are just plain tricky to spell. There's nothing else to do except learn the rules.

Learn the 'i' Before 'e' Rule

Use this rule to decide whether 'i' comes before 'e' or after it:

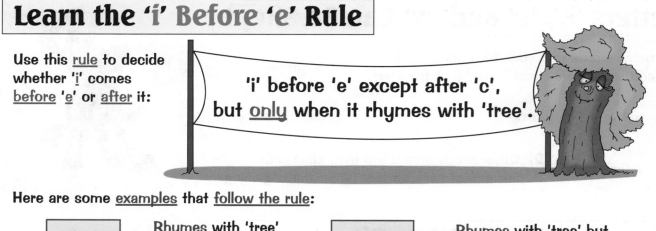

'i' before 'e' except after 'c', but only when it rhymes with 'tree'.

Here are some examples that follow the rule:

relieve ← Rhymes with 'tree' so 'i' before 'e'.

deceive ← Rhymes with 'tree' but follows 'c' so 'i' after 'e'.

science ← Doesn't rhyme with 'tree' but follows 'c' so 'i' before 'e'.

height ← Doesn't rhyme with 'tree' so 'i' after 'e'.

There are exceptions you need to learn.

seize   caffeine   protein ← In these words, the 'ie' sound rhymes with 'tree' but the 'i' comes after 'e'.

Some suffixes break the 'i' before 'e' rule. → spicier   juiciest

Watch Out for Double Letters

Double letters in words can be tricky. Learn these words so you don't trip up in the test.

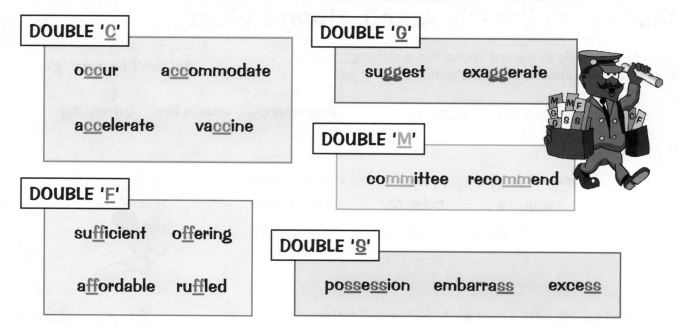

DOUBLE 'C'

occur   accommodate

accelerate   vaccine

DOUBLE 'G'

suggest   exaggerate

DOUBLE 'M'

committee   recommend

DOUBLE 'F'

sufficient   offering

affordable   ruffled

DOUBLE 'S'

possession   embarrass   excess

Section Six — Spelling

Spelling Tricky Words

'ough' Can Be Said in Different Ways

There are loads of different words that have 'ough' in them, and many of these 'ough' words sound very different from one another. Start by learning these ones:

SOUNDS LIKE 'CUFF'	SOUNDS LIKE 'COW'
enough rough	bough plough

SOUNDS LIKE 'SHOW'	SOUNDS LIKE 'SHORT'
dough though	brought thought

SOUNDS LIKE 'NEW'	SOUNDS LIKE 'MOTHER'	SOUNDS LIKE 'OFF'
through	thorough borough	trough

The Letters 'ch' Can Be Said in Different Ways

There are different ways that the letters 'ch' can be pronounced.

1) For most words, they're pronounced like they are in the word 'chair':

> chess   China   ostrich

2) Some 'ch' words sound different, so you need to listen out for them.

SOFT 'CH' The 'ch' in these words is pronounced like the 'sh' in 'shoe'.

> chef   quiche   brochure   charade   moustache

HARD 'CH' In these words, the 'ch' is pronounced like the 'k' in 'kite'.

> echo   orchestra   chorus   character   technology

Spelling Tricky Words

Spelling Vowel Sounds Can Be Tricky

Some <u>vowel sounds</u> aren't spelt how you would <u>usually expect</u>.

1) The 'y' in these words is pronounced like the 'i' in 'tin':

Eg<u>y</u>pt   m<u>y</u>stery   c<u>y</u>gnet   s<u>y</u>mbol   g<u>y</u>m

2) The 'ou' in these words is pronounced like the 'u' in 'bun':

tr<u>ou</u>ble   y<u>ou</u>ng   r<u>ou</u>gh   c<u>ou</u>sin

3) The 'ay' sound is sometimes spelt 'ei', 'eigh' or 'ey':

v<u>ei</u>n   r<u>ei</u>gn   sl<u>eigh</u>   w<u>eigh</u>   gr<u>ey</u>   pr<u>ey</u>

'sc' Can Make an 's' Sound

In some words, the 's' sound like in 'snake' is spelt 'sc'.
Here are some <u>examples</u> for you to learn:

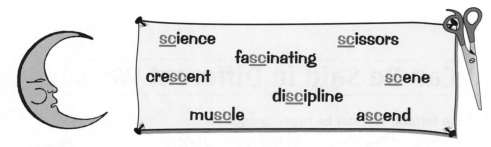

s<u>c</u>ience   s<u>c</u>issors

fas<u>c</u>inating

cres<u>c</u>ent   s<u>c</u>ene

dis<u>c</u>ipline

mus<u>c</u>le   as<u>c</u>end

Look Out For These Exceptions

Most words <u>follow</u> the normal spelling rules, but some words <u>break the rules</u>. You just have to <u>learn</u> these. Here are some <u>common ones</u>:

These are just a few of the words that break spelling rules — there are lots more.

<u>s</u>ure	p<u>eo</u>ple	b<u>u</u>sy	f<u>a</u>ther	br<u>ea</u>k
There is no <u>sh</u> in 'sure'.	There is an <u>eo</u> instead of an <u>ee</u>.	There is no '<u>i</u>' in 'busy'.	It sounds like there is an '<u>ar</u>', but it's spelt '<u>a</u>'.	The '<u>ay</u>' sound is spelt '<u>ea</u>'.

"I can spell tricky words."

Practice Questions

1) One of the words below is spelt incorrectly.
Circle the word and write the **correct** spelling in the box.

disagree   misinformed   automatic   iregular

```
┌─────────────────────────┐
│                         │
└─────────────────────────┘
```

2) Look at the table below. In each row, write the word made by combining the word and **suffix**.

Word	Suffix	New Word
believe	able	
tidy	ness	
access	ible	

3) Look at the words below and tick the word that is spelt **incorrectly**.

Tick **one** box.

frequent   ☐

innocent   ☐

assistant ☐

constent   ☐

4) Draw lines to match each word to its **suffix**.

Word

depend

consider

moist

Suffix

ness

ent

ation

Practice Questions

5) Look at the words below and tick the word that is spelt **incorrectly**.

Tick **one** box.

vigorous ☐

obvious ☐

spontanious ☐

outrageous ☐

6) One of the words below is spelt **incorrectly**.
Circle the word and write the correct spelling in the box.

structure   closure   temperature   fracsure   pleasure

☐

7) Write each of these words with the **correct** spelling.

tention   ....

electrision   ....

submician   ....

actssion   ....

8) Write each of these words with the correct spelling.

ambicious   ....

attracsion   ....

malicios   ....

conscous   ....

expectassion   ....

Practice Questions

9) Read the sentences below. Circle the **correct** word in brackets to complete each sentence.

We went on my friend's computer, but the **(devise / device)** wasn't working.

The amount of traffic on the road will probably **(affect / effect)** our plans.

Shall I **(meet / meat)** you at the restaurant?

10) Look at the words below. For each word, write another word that sounds similar but has a **different spelling**.

dual ....

proceed ....

licence ....

morning ....

11) Complete the sentences below by adding the missing silent letters to the words in bold.

I put the gold watch on my ....**rist** and it started ticking.

We split the pie in **ha**........**f** and ate it between us.

Josie had worked for the **comp**........**ny** for fifteen years.

12) Look at the words below and tick the word that is spelt incorrectly.

Tick **one** box.

multiplied ☐

height ☐

beleive ☐

deceive ☐

Practice Questions

13) One of the words below is spelt incorrectly.
Circle the word and write the correct spelling in the box.

parashute   machine   shoreline   polishing

14) Read the sentences below. Circle the **correct** word in brackets to complete each sentence.

I really love learning about Greek **(mythology / mithology)**.

Beth stood in amazed silence at the base of the **(piramid / pyramid)**.

Do you want **(sirup / syrup)** with your waffles?

15) Look at the words below and tick the word that is spelt incorrectly.

Tick **one** box.

couple   ☐

nurish   ☐

fumble   ☐

country   ☐

16) Write each of these words with the correct spelling.

sucess   ....

apear   ....

throo   ....

coff   ....

shef   ....

tolerent   ....

Glossary

Adjective		A word that describes a noun, e.g. <u>friendly</u> cat, <u>blue</u> pencil.
Adverb		A word that describes a verb, e.g. draw <u>carefully</u>, sing <u>loudly</u>.
Adverbial		A word or group of words which acts like an adverb (it describes a verb), e.g. Sarah went for a run <u>after work</u>.
Antonym		A word that means the <u>opposite</u> to another word, e.g. <u>open</u> and <u>closed</u>.
Apostrophe	**'**	Used to show <u>missing letters</u> and <u>belonging</u> (possession).
Article		The words '<u>the</u>', '<u>a</u>' or '<u>an</u>' which go before a noun. A type of <u>determiner</u>.
Brackets	**( )**	Used to separate <u>extra information</u> in a sentence.
Capital letter	**A**	Used for <u>proper nouns</u> and for <u>starting sentences</u>.
Clause		A bit of a sentence that contains <u>a verb</u> and someone <u>doing the action</u>.
Colon	**:**	Used to introduce some <u>lists</u> and to join <u>sentences</u>.
Comma	**,**	Separates items in a <u>list</u>, separates <u>extra information</u> and <u>joins clauses</u>.
Conjunction		A word or words used to <u>link</u> two <u>clauses</u>, e.g. <u>but</u>, <u>since</u>.
Contracted form		The <u>new word</u> made by <u>joining</u> two words together with an <u>apostrophe</u>.
Co-ordinating conjunction		A word that joins two <u>main clauses</u> in a sentence, e.g. <u>and</u>, <u>or</u>.
Dash	**—**	Used to separate <u>extra information</u> in a sentence or join two <u>main clauses</u> together.
Determiner		A word that goes before a <u>noun</u> to tell you whether it is <u>general</u> or <u>specific</u>.
Direct speech		The <u>actual</u> words that are <u>said</u> by someone.
Exclamation mark	**!**	Used to show strong <u>feelings</u> and for some <u>commands</u>.
Full stop		Used to show where a sentence <u>ends</u>.

74

Glossary

Homophones		Words that <u>sound the same</u> but have <u>different meanings</u>, e.g. <u>pair</u> and <u>pear</u>.
Inverted commas	" "	Used to show <u>direct speech</u>.
Main clause		An <u>important</u> bit of a sentence that would <u>make sense</u> on its own, e.g. <u>They cleaned</u> before they left. 'They cleaned' is the <u>main clause</u>.
Noun		A word that <u>names</u> something, e.g. <u>David</u>, <u>scissors</u>, <u>swarm</u>, <u>jealousy</u>.
Noun phrase		A group of words which includes a noun and any words that describe it, e.g. Johan opened <u>the heavy old door at the top of the stairs</u>.
Parenthesis		Part of a sentence that gives <u>extra information</u>. It is <u>separated</u> from the rest of the sentence by <u>brackets</u>, <u>dashes</u> or <u>commas</u>.
Phrase		A <u>small part</u> of a sentence, usually <u>without a verb</u>.
Prefix		<u>Letters</u> that can be put <u>in front</u> of a word to change its meaning, e.g. <u>re</u>heat.
Preposition		A word that tells you <u>how</u> things are <u>related</u>, e.g. <u>under</u>, <u>across</u>, <u>during</u>.
Pronoun		A word that can be used <u>instead of a noun</u>, e.g. <u>I</u>, <u>he</u>, <u>we</u>, <u>they</u>.
Question mark	?	Used at the end of <u>questions</u>.
Semi-colon	;	Used to separate <u>lists</u> of longer things and to <u>join</u> sentences.
Subjunctive form		A verb form that appears in <u>formal</u> writing, e.g. If I <u>were</u> you, I would do it.
Subordinate clause		A <u>less important</u> bit of a sentence which <u>doesn't make sense</u> on its own, e.g. <u>Although I ran</u>, I was late. 'Although I ran' is the <u>subordinate clause</u>.
Subordinating conjunction		A word or group of words which joins a <u>main clause</u> to a <u>subordinate clause</u>, e.g. <u>even though</u>, <u>because</u>.
Suffix		Letters that can be put <u>after</u> a word to change its meaning, e.g. help<u>er</u>.
Synonym		A word with <u>the same</u> or a <u>similar meaning</u> to another word, e.g. <u>happy</u> and <u>cheerful</u>.
Verb		A <u>doing</u> or <u>being</u> word, e.g. you <u>go</u>, it <u>flies</u>, she <u>hops</u>.

Glossary

Answers

Pages 10-19 — Section One: Reading

The Coral Island

1) So they can get a better look at the boat.

2) quickly

3) It shows they are excited.

4) Ralph says that he loved Coral Island, but that he would have gone back home in an instant.

5) The pirates have fired the cannon.

6) crashing / carried away several cocoa-nut trees / burst in atoms

7) The ship's flag has a skull and crossbones on it.

8) E.g. He has a grave, anxious expression, showing he cares about his friends.
He comes up with a plan quickly.
His friends follow him.

9) circuitous / halted / cautiously / glanced

10) false
false
true
true
false

11) At first they are excited to see the boat and they want the boat to see them. Later they are desperate to avoid the boat because they do not want the pirates to find them.

12) E.g. The text says that the boys are high on the cliffs and taking care not to be spotted, so Jack's plan might work and they might avoid being noticed by the pirates.

Libraries

1) Libraries have a more interesting and important history than people think.

2) It is famous.

3) E.g. It held 700,000 books from all over the world.

4) elaborate, fancily decorated

5) 1. Some people thought it would be too costly.
2. Others didn't like the idea of giving people something for nothing.

6) E.g. Alexandria mainly held scrolls and Manchester held books.
Alexandria held more books than Manchester.
Alexandria was looked after by a king while Manchester was looked after by a former bricklayer.

7) It simplified the process of organising and locating books.

8) a household name / illustrious

9) Information is easy to find on the internet. / Cheap books can be ordered over the internet.

10) attract people by offering them something

11) E.g. Normal library use may continue falling, but libraries can innovate to attract new users.

12) 6 There is still hope for libraries.
4 Several famous people worked in libraries.
1 A description of the first libraries.
3 A new system to organise books is described.
5 An explanation for the decline of library use.
2 A description of the Public Libraries Act.

The Superstitious Ghost

1) demure / inoffensive / apprehensive / cower / fearful

2) hides in bed

3) human beings

4) E.g. Humans walk, ghosts glide.
Humans are solid, ghosts are see-through.

5) It makes the reader feel scared of them.

6) strange

7) E.g. Humans have a physical form which is different to ghosts, which makes them scary.
Humans waste their time doing things that don't matter.
In the same way humans can be 'scared to death' ghosts can be scared 'quite alive'.

Answers

Pages 27-29 — Section Two: Word Types

1) Example of using handle as a noun:
The **handle** of the metal spoon felt very hot.
Example of using handle as a verb:
Mr. Jacobs didn't know how to **handle** the situation.
   In the first part of the answer, the handle needs to be a thing. In the second part of the answer, someone in the sentence needs to be handling something.

2) The **excitement** of seeing a **pod** of **whales** made **Starr** jump for **joy**. She grabbed her **camera** and started to film.

3) There might be a thunderstorm tonight.

4) The modal verb 'might' changes the second sentence to make it less likely Rosina and her brother play squash with their cousin.

5) powerful / powerless
noisy / noiseless
energetic
adventurous

6) adverb
adjective
adjective

7) Her dress is __quite__ ugly, so __maybe__ she'll buy a different one __tomorrow__.

8) Before work, I had to go to an appointment.
   The adverbial must be followed by a comma.

9) Emil had to go to the doctor **because of** his sore knee.
Alison was eating sweets **throughout** the exam.
The new post office is **beside** the butcher's.

10) theirs
mine
ours

11) The restaurant **which** Sanjay and Imogen like was recently given an award. It's the same award **that** the restaurant next door got last year.

12) I have to sew **some** buttons onto **this** jacket.
Isla has **fifteen** hens, but **that** hen is **her** favourite.

Pages 41-43 — Section Three: Sentences and Tenses

1) "They're going to the museum today, **aren't they**?"

2) E.g. Rory dropped the box of eggs **while he was shopping**.
   If the subordinate clause is added before the main clause, it must be followed by a comma.

3) E.g. the tranquil pond in the park

4) co-ordinating
subordinating
subordinating

5) Joseph and his grandpa built the model aeroplanes.

6) By the time Sophie arrived, the flight **had** left.

7) I **needed** to repair the hole in my jumper, so my uncle **taught** me to sew.

8) was staring
was stalking

9) Her brother wasn't too fussed.

10) E.g. untidy

11) It is necessary that he sign the document.

12) The rabbit jumped around on the lawn **quickly**.
You can exchange the CD for **those** DVDs on the table.

13) Non-Standard English
Non-Standard English
Standard English
Standard English

Pages 52-53 — Section Four: Punctuation

1) Once she'd been to the gym**,** the swimmer went home to have lunch with her parents.

2) After eating their lunch, the children went to play basketball in the playground.

3) Karis climbed a mountain with her brother, Andrew**,** and the dog.

4) I told my friends that I didn't want to go to the house that's on the hill (Lady Bowsprit lives there with her **son's** dogs), but they made me go there anyway. We went at nine o'clock after the sun went down.

Answers

5) "Don't go over there!" shouted Mabel. "**T**here's a bear hiding behind that tree."

6) incorrect
   incorrect
   incorrect
   correct

7) I found three rooms in the castle: the kitchen (which had seven ovens) was on the ground floor; the library was on the first floor; and the master bedroom was at the top of the highest tower.

8) When he travelled to the rainforest (which was in Peru), Mr Riddle learned lots about the animals that lived there.

9) The three-storey building up the street nearly collapsed last night.

10) The fast-talking donkey managed to get himself out of trouble.

Page 58 — Section Five: Vocabulary

1) taken apart from each other.
   connected together again.

2) ity, ise
   Using these two suffixes, you can make the words 'publicity' and 'publicise'.

3) E.g. bicycle, unicycle, cycling

4) a) A word with the same or very similar meaning to another word.
   b) E.g. envious

5) E.g. tense, nervous
   E.g. humble, modest

Pages 69-72 — Section Six: Spelling

1) **iregular** should be spelled **irregular**

2) believable
   tidiness
   accessible

3) **constent** should be spelled **constant**

4) depend — ent
   consider — ation
   moist — ness

5) **spontanious** should be spelled **spontaneous**

6) **fracsure** should be spelled **fracture**

7) tension
   electrician
   submission
   action

8) ambitious
   attraction
   malicious
   conscious
   expectation

9) We went on my friend's computer, but the **device** wasn't working.
   The amount of traffic on the road will probably **affect** our plans.
   Shall I **meet** you at the restaurant?

10) duel
    precede
    license
    mourning

11) I put the gold watch on my **wrist** and it started ticking.
    We split the pie in half and ate it between us.
    Josie had worked for the company for fifteen years.

12) **beleive** should be spelled **believe**

13) **parashute** should be spelled **parachute**

14) I really love learning about Greek **mythology**.
    Beth stood in amazed silence at the base of the **pyramid**.
    Do you want **syrup** with your waffles?

15) **nurish** should be spelled **nourish**

16) success
    appear
    through
    cough
    chef
    tolerant

Index

E6HR23